Mohawk

Blood

Mohawk Blood

...

Michael Baughman

LYONS & BURFORD, PUBLISHERS

PRINTED IN THE UNITED STATES OF AMERICA
DESIGN BY KATHY KIKKERT
ILLUSTRATIONS BY MICHAEL MUSTO
10 9 8 7 6 5 4 3 2 1

LIBRARY OF CONGRESS CATALOGING-IN-PUBLICATION DATA

BAUGHMAN, MIKE.
MOHAWK BLOOD : A NATIVE AMERICAN QUEST / MICHAEL BAUGHMAN.
P.   CM.
ISBN 1-55821-376-7
1. BRANT, JOSEPH, 1742–1807.   2. BAUGHMAN, MIKE.
3. MOHAWK INDIANS — BIOGRAPHY.   4. MOHAWK INDIANS —
ETHNIC IDENTITY. 5. BRANT, JOSEPH, 1742–1807. I. TITLE
E99.M8B383   1995
973'.04973'0092 — DC20
[B]   94-37289
CIP

Contents

Foreword

The two most important people in these narratives are the Mohawk war chief Thayendanegea, who became known as Joseph Brant, and my great-grandfather, John Brant, who taught me about Joseph. Even though John Brant died when I was a boy, most of what I consider valuable in my life has been a direct result of his companionship and his example.

Perhaps the most difficult part of putting this short book together was deciding what to leave out. Hemingway may have been the first American author to discuss the importance of carefully selective exclusion, and I think he was quite right about it: by telling less, sometimes it's possible to say more, and to say it more clearly. So there isn't much here about my various jobs, which have ranged from dish washing to college teaching. Certainly some jobs are better than others—it's often more fun to be an English professor than a private in the army—but all my occupations have been, to a large degree, the concessions I've made to a culture increasingly dominated by sterile technology and preoccupied with acquiring money and the often-useless things it can buy.

.

I've also left out many of the most pleasant experiences of my life, even though they relate clearly to my subject. There's no mention of calm early mornings spent kayaking on the Sea of Cortez with schools of bottle-nosed dolphins for company; or of a January night my wife Hilde and I cross-country skied through the Cascade Mountains under the light of a full moon with a pack of coyotes howling close behind us; or of watching a Florida panther slink across a clearing in the woods, and then, that same evening, collecting lobsters for dinner in knee-deep water on the Keys; or of surfing on hand-carved eighty-pound redwood boards in Hawaii; or of watching my daughter Ingrid land her first summer steelhead on the fly, a bright twelve-pound native female from our favorite (unnamed) river.

There isn't a lot here about my family, either, even though they are without question the best luck I've had in life. But, in an important way, their influence is what made me want to write this book in the first place, and that's why I could leave out so much about them. I'm a man in his mid-fifties, the father of grown children, a recent grandfather, and I finally have the feeling I can relate what has mattered to me, why it matters and what it means—for them.

Both Joseph and John Brant tried to live in the cultures they found themselves in—what intelligent choice do any of us have about that?—and at the same time preserve as much of Mohawk life *as they practically could*. I've tried that, too, and I hope my children, and their children, do the same—and even though it becomes more difficult with each generation, I believe it's still quite possible they'll succeed.

The only advice I have for them is recorded here.

·

If a man loses anything and goes back and looks carefully for it, he will find it.

——SITTING BULL

Prologue

... they [our American Indians] are poor people. They live in shacks, drive secondhand Oldsmobiles and eat too much Wonder Bread. The reasons for this deplorable situation are many, varied and complicated, as any sociologist can explain to you, but basically it comes down to the fact, observed all over the world, that the descendants of hunters and warriors do not make good clerk typists or computer tapers.

———EDWARD ABBEY, *THE JOURNEY HOME*

On my lonely drive down out of South Dakota's Black Hills, I saw deer and elk, and a large herd of buffalo. Most of the cows were nursing calves in the early morning light. Not long after I reached what locals call the "prairie," I passed a sign that told me I was entering the Pine Ridge Reservation. A healthy coyote trotted across the lonely two-lane road a hundred yards ahead of me—he stopped just long enough to turn only his head and watch me pass—and then I saw a small herd of pronghorn antelope grazing up a gently sloping rise of new spring grass.

·

On the other side of the long rise, not far from Oglala, I
hit some bottomland—thick brush with big old cottonwoods in fresh green leaf—and I parked off the road,
locked the car, and hiked south along the creek bed. It
looked like a place for turkeys and, wearing a camouflage
shirt and hat, I made my way along slowly and as quietly as
possible, staying concealed and yelping with a mouth-
diaphragm call every hundred yards or so. I hadn't gone a
mile when a gobbler answered loudly from eighty or ninety
yards away. This was a mature old Merriams, but appar-
ently without hens and not particularly wary, because
within minutes, answering with a soft yelp every time he
gobbled, I had called him in to thirty-five or forty yards.
Huge tail fanned, wattles fiery red in slanting sunlight,
head white as polished ivory, and ten-inch beard clearly visible against his iridescent breast feathers, he strutted back

and forth on a small, dusty patch of earth between two of
the cottonwood trees. I watched him for a quarter of an
hour, talking to him the whole time, until he finally tired of
the game and walked off, slowly and with no loss of dignity,
back toward wherever he had come from.

The next couple of hours weren't so happy. In Pine
Ridge itself, I saw the old cars and the run-down shacks
that Abbey mentions, the stray dogs, the poverty, the clear
human signs of poor nutrition and bad health. Despair is a
strongly palpable thing in that place, and I talked to the
man I had come to see and left immediately afterward.

North of Pine Ridge, I stopped at Wounded Knee. I was
standing alone in a cool north wind, reading the sign
describing the massacre, when another old car, sputtering
and backfiring, clanking and lurching, approached from
the north. (This one wasn't an Oldsmobile, but a Pontiac.)

It rolled to a slow stop beside my embarrassingly new
and shiny rental, and two old men got out. Immediately
they reminded me of the large black-and-white pho-
tographs that are on prominent display at the Rapid City
airport—photos taken in the 1930s showing Sioux sur-
vivors of the Little Big Horn battle. These two had the
same lean and erect bodies, the same dark faces deeply
creased from long, hard lives. The only difference was that
they were dressed not as warriors but as hunters, in tattered
old camouflage. They waved at me, barely moving their
hands. When I waved back, barely moving my hand, both
expressionless faces suddenly smiled.

They walked up slowly and stood just behind me as I
finished reading the sign. None of us said anything because
there isn't very much left to say about Wounded Knee. The

•

only sound was the steady wind coming down out of the badlands.

"Hunting?" I said to them after a decent interval.

"Turkeys," one of them answered.

"No slow elk?" I asked.

"Slow elk" is what Indians often call white men's cattle, and they both laughed quietly at the old joke.

"Not so many birds this year," said one. "Bad nesting last spring. Too much cold and rain."

"But enough birds," said the other. "We got a good one in the trunk."

They showed it to me, as heavy a Merriams as I've ever seen, with inch-and-a-quarter–long spurs and two good beards. Then they showed me their wing-bone calls and their ancient single-shot twelve-gauge guns. They told how they had roosted the big gobbler the night before, camped nearby, then set up and called it in at first light in the morning. Now they were on their way to another good place where they would hunt some more, moving slowly and calling with their wing bones to locate gobblers, as I had done on the bottomland near Oglala.

For a while at least, they were free and proud and happy.

1

. . .

John Brant

I grew up in a house on a lonely dirt road a few miles outside Jeanette, Pennsylvania. Thick woods began where the
backyard ended, and I explored there as often as I could, in
all seasons, looking for birds and animals, sometimes fol-

.

lowing their tracks through winter snow. I flushed pheasants from among the trees where they roosted at night, and was frightened every time by the sudden, powerful drumming of wings and the crowing of the brightly colored, long-tailed roosters. There were red and gray squirrels, rabbits, porcupines, skunks, raccoons, occasional deer, and I was sure I saw a bear once, huge and black, crashing out of a patch of brush and then disappearing over a hill; but no one at home or at school would believe me.

For a boy who hated being indoors it was a good enough place to live, but my trips to my Great-grandfather John Brant's farm southeast of Jeanette near the Allegheny Mountains were the happiest times of my young life. He lived along a dirt road, too, in a square white two-story house surrounded by apple trees. About a hundred yards behind the house was a large barn, and a trail led from there over a hill and down through oak trees to a fair-sized trout stream. I think its waters are now used to irrigate a golf course, but in those days they held brown trout that were very tough to catch. I landed a few small ones using worms for bait—I remember the cold, slippery feel of their writhing bodies—and I watched Granddad Brant, late at night, by moonlight, when he sometimes pulled fat golden, speckled fish as long as my arm out of the darkest waters of the deepest pools.

He was a tough old man, with broad shoulders, a narrow waist, and powerful arms that looked like brown leather stretched over networks of cables and wires. About the time he was teaching me to shoot and fish, when he was well into his seventies, he had to have his appendix removed. After two days in the hospital, he insisted on

·

going home, and the day after that, when his son Noss, a doctor himself, came to the farm to visit and check up, he found Granddad Brant back behind the barn loading sacks of grain onto a wagon.

As far as I was concerned, the barn was a much more interesting and comfortable place than the house. It was bigger than the house, too; another square building made solidly of raw planks and smelling strongly and pleasantly of hay, dried-out wood, manure, oil, and leather. Everything in the building was organized neatly: plows in two corners, rakes and pitchforks against the back wall, harness hung on shiny nails, and hand tools—planes, saws, wrenches, hammers, screwdrivers, drills, wire cutters, pliers—arranged in wooden compartments along the wall between the plows. There were small kegs of nails, nuts and bolts, and, in a dark corner, three axes with taped handles, their heads shiny from use, were driven into a thick

tree stump. I tried to pull those axes out at least once during every visit, but I couldn't ever do it.

Granddad Brant also kept bourbon in the barn because his wife didn't want it in the house. (I know it was bourbon because I still remember the distinctive smell that blended so nicely with those other heavy odors.) But the only time he sipped the bourbon was when he told me about our ancestor, Chief Joseph Brant of the Mohawks.

Most of the times we spent in the barn together were about the same, but I remember one afternoon more clearly than all the others. The path from the house was lined on both sides with red raspberry bushes, and I had collected a hatful of the ripe berries on the walk out. By the time I arrived, my fingers already stained red from juice, Grand-dad Brant was hard at work, measuring, sawing and plan-ing, making a table. One of the things that impressed me most about him—and it still does—was the fact that he seemed able to do nearly everything. I knew he had built the barn. I had watched him make his own boots and shoes. He worked on pipes and wires, installed doors and win-dows, repaired machines, skinned animals, trained dogs, served as the area's veterinarian, tied trout flies, and made his own fishing rods, too. (He built me a rocking chair for my first birthday, and I still have it, as solid as if it were new, ready to be used by my grandson.)

Usually I sat on an overturned keg to watch him work. He nearly always wore a clean white shirt tucked into baggy trousers held up by suspenders, but somehow his clothes never seemed to get dirty, no matter what he did. I was wondering how he kept his clothes so clean and think-ing about some recent problems at home as I ate raspberries

·

that day, but I didn't say anything until after I'd finished the
berries.

"I got in trouble," I told him then.

"Because you told people you saw a bear?"

"I did see one. But it wasn't that. I got in a fight."

"I think it was a bear you saw." He was using a pencil
and a yardstick to draw a line along a smooth white board.
"Who'd you fight with? When did it happen?"

"My cousin Bob, about three weeks ago."

"The fat one. Tell me about it."

I told him because he always listened to whatever I said
without interrupting, and he always had something kind
and helpful to say about it afterward. I don't remember
how much detail I included, but this is what had happened:

In Jeanette I had two cousins on my father's side, one a
year older and one a year younger, and on many Saturday
mornings in summer, with fifty cents apiece in our pockets,
we walked downtown to watch cowboy movies together.
The most memorable part of the walk was the long bridge
over the railroad tracks leading into town, where there was
little to see in any direction but dirt, soot, concrete, and
steel. (And sometimes a small plane flew overhead, writing
"Coca-Cola" or "Pepsi-Cola" in bright white smoke in the
sky.) Usually I lagged behind Bob and Chuck and listened
to them talk about the various cowboy stars: Roy Rogers,
Gene Autry, Hopalong Cassidy, Tom Mix. Sometimes they
argued loudly over which one was the best cowboy of the
bunch.

The dark theater, full of noisy kids, and with the smell
of popcorn and the sound of candy wrappers, seemed nicer
than the town. There was always a newsreel, and we booed

•

and jeered at the Germans and Japanese. Next came a short or a cartoon, or, if we were very lucky, both. We liked The Three Stooges, Bugs Bunny, and Donald Duck. We hated Casper the Friendly Ghost and jeered him almost as angrily as we did Hitler. The cowboy movies were always the same, no matter who was in them. And when Indians were included, they were always the same, too. There was never any indication of how they hunted animals and birds and caught fish to feed themselves, or of how they lived together as families and raised their children. They were screaming, bloodthirsty savages with feathers on their heads and painted faces, and the kids cheered happily when they suffered their presumably well-deserved defeats. I didn't cheer, though. Even at that age, I sat and wondered what the country outside had been like—the crowded neighborhoods, the noisy streets, the dirty bridge over railroad tracks—before the white men came, before there were any cowboys. I wondered exactly who and what the kids were cheering. (I also wondered—and still do—why it was supposed to be important, or even interesting, when someone stood in front of a camera pretending to be somebody else.)

Back in their yard after the movies, Bob and Chuck usually wanted to play cowboys and Indians. I was always the Indian, but I refused to be defeated. Finally, after this had happened half a dozen times or more, I ended up in a real fight with Bob, who was the oldest. I won the fight—I punched him with both hands, got a headlock on him, tossed him onto his back, and pinned him and made him quit—but both Bob's father and mine were angry at me, and despite my mother's pleading my father spanked my bare bottom hard with a yardstick. It was watching Grand-

•

dad Brant draw his line with a yardstick that made me remember and want to tell him about it.

When I finished talking, he looked up from his work. "Did the spanking hurt a lot?"

"Not too much," I said.

"It wouldn't, it wouldn't." When his dark face smiled, the wrinkles disappeared, and his teeth were as white as his thick hair. "I think your parents are afraid you're a little too wild. I think that's why they punish you sometimes. Come on. Let's sit in the corner a while."

I carried my small keg over to the corner, which was

where he kept his bourbon, on a shelf above the larger keg he used as a stool. Besides the bourbon, there were empty jars and bottles on the shelf, a clean clear-glass tumbler turned upside down, and a yellowed human skull. Grand-dad Brant had told me it was a Mohawk skull, and after he'd poured some bourbon into the tumbler, he put the bottle back on the shelf and picked up the skull.

"How old is it?" I asked him.

"Oh, about a hundred and fifty years."

"Is it the chief's?"

At that he looked at me and chuckled, his shoulders shaking silently, the skull in one big hand and his bourbon in the other. "It just might be," he said. "It's possible, Mikey. Here!"

I took the skull and held it. I loved to feel its cool, smooth solidity.

He took his first sip, smacked his lips, and smiled as he looked at the tumbler. I smelled the bourbon and sat there holding the skull and watching him. "You are a little wild," he began. "And that's good. A little fighting isn't so bad. I don't think I ever told you that Joseph Brant was a good wrestler. So good he fought lots of matches in front of the whites, the way boxers fight in front of crowds now. Later on, when he was a war chief, a lot of people thought he was the best fighter alive. After the war, he was still a chief, and he was educated—he'd been to school and spoke some languages besides English—but he always loved his hunting and fishing and did it whenever he could, all his life. He was a Mohawk, and he loved being one; but he knew he and his people had to live in a white world, whether they wanted to or not. You'll have to, also. Do you know what I mean?"

·

"I think so. Sure."

He took another sip of his bourbon and smiled at the glass again. "It doesn't even matter if you understand everything I say, Mikey, just so you remember it. You'll understand it someday. Remember this—not even animals can live anymore if they're *too* wild."

"How come?"

"It's pretty complicated. A long time ago, there were wolves around here. Did you know that?"

"Real wolves?"

"The big ones weighed one hundred pounds, more than you do. You know how big my dogs' tracks are. A wolf's tracks would be three times as big."

"What happened to them?"

"People killed a lot of them, and the rest died off. Wolves could only live in wild places; that was their prob-

lem. Grizzly bears, too. Deer don't mind people so much. Black bears don't, either. Dogs are related to wolves, and they like people a lot. That's because they've been around people so much, their wildness is almost gone. Wolves are better animals—stronger animals—but a lot more dogs are alive. Maybe Mohawks were better people in some ways, but a lot more whites are alive."

"It sounds pretty complicated to me."

"It is, it is. Let me try to tell you one more important thing about it, and then we'll take a walk. As soon as I finish with this"—he held the glass up between us—"we'll take a walk down to the creek. It's a good day for it. Okay?"

"Sure!"

"This is pretty complicated, but try to remember. The reason the Mohawks had good lives—the reason they got along and were mostly happy before the whites came—was *because* they had to live in the wild. When life is hard work for everybody, and dangerous lots of times, too, nobody worries about things that don't matter. People get along with one another—they help one another—because if they didn't, they couldn't stay alive. See what I mean?"

"Sure, I understand that," I said, and I did.

"Well, nowadays life isn't very hard or very dangerous, except for the people in the war, and the war's almost over. Joseph Brant understood it all a long time ago. He understood that some modern things from the whites were good, but that the Mohawks should try to keep some of their old ways, too. Some of their *wild* ways. How do you keep wild ways in a world full of people and machines? That was the problem. It still is. It's a bigger problem than ever today. It keeps getting bigger all the time."

·

His hand on my shoulder, we walked across a field, up a hill through the shade of oak trees, then down the other side of the hill toward the creek. I could hear the moving water before we saw it. "There's a hatch on," Granddad Brant said. "Lots of flies on the water. We'll see some trout today."

When we reached the creek, he made me stay behind him, and he sneaked along the bank, looking through the brush at the water. "Here's a good place," he finally said. "See the big one over there on the far side?"

The calm, dark water of the pool we were watching was marked by the rings of many feeding trout, but I didn't know which one he meant. "Where?" I asked him.

"Right beside the old log in the water. Down at the bottom end of the log. See it?"

"Now I do."

All I could actually see was the dark, wavering form in the water, barely moving, inches beneath the surface. Every so often, no more than two or three times in a minute, the big fish would suddenly become more visible as it rose. Then another ring would show and drift downstream to disappear in the shallow, faster water where the creek narrowed at a bend. The trout never moved from side to side, but fed only on the flies that floated directly over the lie. We watched for what seemed like a long time.

"He's the biggest one in this pool," Granddad Brant said. "Do you want to get a closer look?"

"How?"

"Do you think you can be patient?"

"Maybe. I think so."

"I think you're old enough to try. The Mohawks didn't

•

have all the things that people use now to help them when they fish and hunt. They didn't have gasoline engines and binoculars and rifles to do their work for them. When they had to use bows and arrows and spears, they learned a lot— a lot of things hardly anybody learns anymore. But you can still learn if you want to, if you try. This is a good hatch. It'll keep on going for at least another hour. Do you really know what patience is?"

"Sort of, I guess."

"It means you have to be calm. Not complain, even when something is hard. Even when something hurts. Lots of times you have to be patient to get something good done. I'll show you what I mean. Watch now. Watch the big trout."

He took his hand from my shoulder and ran it through the grass and leaves behind us until he found a small stone. "Watch that trout," he said, and when he tossed the stone across the creek, and it landed with a small splash near the log, the big fish suddenly disappeared.

"Did you see where it went?" he asked me.

"No. I didn't see anything."

"He went downstream and out toward the middle. I think he stopped down there right before the shallow water starts. Now here's what you need to do, Mikey. Walk upstream and cross over where you can—you can swim, I'll keep an eye on you—and then walk down the bank over there, nice and slow, and wade in right above the log. Then stand there right out from the log, just a couple of feet from where the trout was before I threw the stone. If you can stand there long enough, and you stay still enough, really still, he'll come back to feed in the same place again. That

·

way you can see him from up close. You'll be right next to him. Go ahead now. Try it."

I walked up the bank and crossed, then came back down the other side, waded out, the rubber soles of my sneakers slipping on rocks, and stood near the log. The cold water, pushing steadily against me, reached halfway up my thighs.

"Don't move your arms," Granddad Brant called across to me. "Don't move your head, either. Don't move *anything*. You can do it."

I stood there for a few minutes, staring at the place in the stream where the trout had been. Flies—they might have been mayflies—had begun landing on my face and arms.

"Don't move!" Granddad Brant called to me again. "Don't move *anything*!"

I'd tried to brush the flies away from my face, but I didn't try again.

The water became unpleasantly cold, numbing my legs, and more and more of the flies crawled across my face and up and down my bare arms, but I stood there for a long time, absolutely motionless. Then something magical happened. After a while, I no longer noticed the water. The flies, though thicker all the time, didn't bother me, either. Somehow I realized that they belonged to this place, and because they did there wasn't any reason they should bother me—not if I belonged to the place, too, as I wanted to belong. Trees shaded the cold water, and trout fed on the flies on the water. And I had become a part of it all.

I didn't see where it came from, but the trout was suddenly back, close beside my leg, moving slightly, undulating, nosing into the steady current.

.

·

"You did it, Mikey!" Granddad Brant called. "Don't move! Stay nice and still!"

Nothing could have made me move, and soon the trout began to feed again. The small flies floated down, dark-bodied with light-colored wings, some of them struggling on the water, and it was always the struggling flies that the trout came up for. Between flies the trout held a few inches beneath the surface, long golden-brown speckle-backed body undulating slightly, fins occasionally wavering in the current, and I knew for certain it was the most wonderful thing I'd ever seen.

I stood until the hatch of flies ended; and as soon as it did, the trout immediately disappeared again, gone some-where into the deeper, darker water of the pool.

"Time to go," Granddad Brant called across, and when I looked at him I realized that it was nearly dark. He must have known what I'd felt. We didn't talk the whole way home.

Both my mother and Grandma Brant were mad—or at least visibly irritated—when we finally reached the house. We were late for dinner by quite a while. Besides, one of Granddad Brant's springer spaniels, a young male named Pat, my favorite, had turned up with a mouth and snout full of porcupine quills.

"Where is he?" Granddad Brant asked.

"Out in the barn," his wife answered. "I put him in the first horse stall on a blanket. Aren't you going to eat?"

"You go ahead. Don't wait for me," he said, and he headed back outside.

·

"Can I go, too?" I asked, and started out after him.

"You eat your dinner," my mother answered.

I got my dinner down in three or four minutes, refused dessert, and hurried outside. A light showed through the open barn door and the windows on either side, and when I ran in I saw that Granddad Brant had hung a lantern from a wire and had Pat on a blanket directly underneath it.

Standing quietly behind him, I watched over his shoulder. The dog, on its side, legs curled tightly, panted and whined. The quills looked long and slender in the light, protruding from his nose, from his jaw, even from his swollen tongue, which hung from the side of his mouth. Foam, pink with blood, bubbled out of his nose when he breathed.

Granddad Brant had one hand pressed against the dog's shoulder, while he picked out the quills with his other hand. He worked quickly, but gently, too, and each time he pulled out a quill, a small spot of bright red blood marked the spot. Beside the dog was a bottle half full of what looked like bourbon, and after every four or five quills he removed, Granddad Brant carefully poured a little on the wounds.

"What's that?" I asked.

"Vinegar. There's something in it that helps. Go back to the house, Mikey, and bring me some water in a bucket and some towels. Clean towels. Old but clean."

"Will he be okay?"

"He'll be okay. It didn't happen long ago, so the quills haven't buried themselves yet. Go on, now."

I ran back to the house and brought the bucket of water and towels. It took Granddad Brant at least an hour to get all the quills out, and afterward he washed the wounds carefully and stroked Pat's side. Pat was breathing easily

·

now, no longer whining, and his legs had relaxed. "You'll be fine, boy," Granddad Brant told him. "Maybe you learned something from it. I hope so. But you'll be fine."

Granddad Brant looked back over his shoulder at me. "This is what can happen when a tame animal runs into a wild one," he said. "You'd better go on back to the house. They must be waiting."

"Aren't you coming?"

He didn't come back to the house. He spent the night with Pat in the barn.

Granddad was strong, kind, and brave, too.

I went with my mother to visit him just before he died, and late one evening—I remember that it was nearly dark, with the branches of apple trees silhouetted against a gray sky just outside the window—I talked with him for ten or fifteen minutes. The bedroom smelled strongly of varnish and clean sheets, not nearly as appealing as the familiar odors I knew from the barn.

We were all alone, and he surely knew he was dying and probably knew it would happen within hours. He smiled and talked about the fish and animals we'd seen together, and he told me the .22 rifle I'd learned to shoot was mine.

He lay there propped up, sometimes laughing as he talked, arms and big hands at his sides, lined face dark brown in contrast to his white hair and the clean pillow. He told me never to let them take the wildness out of me—that was when he laughed—and he told me to keep learning to hunt and fish. He told me not to forget the things he'd talked to me about, and not to cry.

·

·

Early the next morning, after I learned he had died, I looked for the skull in the barn. But it had disappeared, and no one I asked later knew what had happened to it; or if they knew, they wouldn't tell me. The bottle on the shelf still held a few inches of bourbon, and I pulled out the cork to sniff it, but I didn't have the nerve to try a sip.

Standing there alone in the barn, smelling the hay and wood, the manure and oil and leather, I knew I would remember.

·

2

. . .

Cowboys

and Indians

Again

Not long after John Brant died, my mother and father left
Pennsylvania; and, like so many Americans in the years just
after the war, headed west in search of better jobs and a better place. We spent time in Texas, California, and then

.

Hawaii, where I graduated from high school in 1955. After a year at Boston University on a football scholarship, I quit school and headed west again. In fact, for the next several years, I headed in every direction. Often.

Hitchhiking, occasionally riding Greyhound buses, hopping freights, even walking as far as thirty or forty miles at a time, I visited every state, many of them more than once. Motivated both by youthful restlessness and curiosity, my purpose was to learn as much as I could about this huge and complicated country, to see what I was getting into and learn to avoid as much of it as I could. Working at odd and always-low-paying jobs, sleeping in cheap rooms—or in bus stations or parks or all-night diners, or on lonely beaches or small-town airport runways or plowed fields—I would last a week or two in a place, sometimes a month or more, and then, with a little money saved, move on.

It was New York City that finally headed me west for the last time.

My job there had something to do with it. This was in the fall, and on my first day in town, I walked into Macy's department store (I'd heard it was the largest in the world), found the personnel department, and asked a secretary if they needed help. She didn't actually answer me or even look at me, but she shoved an application form across the counter. Fifteen or twenty minutes after I'd filled it out, I found myself in a small, windowless room, furnished with an institutional metal desk and a single chair, being interviewed by a sad-eyed bald man in a rumpled suit.

At first I thought the interview was going very well and even had visions of some sort of responsible position.

"I see you've had some college," he said in an almost-

·

friendly tone, looking over the top of the application at me. "How were your grades?"

"Fine. I didn't flunk out or anything. My grades were good. I just didn't have any idea what I wanted to major in."

He nodded and seemed to almost smile. "One thing you'll have to do is shave that beard."

"Fine," I answered. "I don't mind that. I was going to shave it off anyway."

He went back to the application, frowning slightly as he read it. On it, as a reference, I'd included the name of Henry J. Kaiser, the well-known industrialist and financier for whom I'd worked in Hawaii one summer, cleaning and painting his swimming pool.

Though the interviewer didn't ask about Mr. Kaiser, after a few more questions, he offered me a job—but not the kind I'd imagined, and it didn't have much to do with a clean shave.

There had been a sale, during which thousands of women's left shoes had been displayed in Macy's store windows. Meanwhile, the right shoes had been dumped into a pile on the stockroom floor. When the sale ended, the left shoes were dumped in on top of the rights, and I was hired to rematch the pairs and put them in boxes.

For eight hours a day, with half an hour for lunch (always one hot dog and a large orange drink at the nearby Nedick's), I crawled and pawed through stiff, shiny leather in the dusty gloom of a concrete basement. Against one wall was a towering stack of white cardboard shoe boxes. After I had a pair back together, I had to find the correctly marked box to put them in, and place that box against the wall to the right of the empties. Every hour or two, my

·

immediate boss—another bald man, this one with glasses and a black mustache—came by from the shoe department to see that I was working. He never spoke to me, but each time he visited, he opened up a couple of boxes at random to make sure the shoes inside were matched correctly.

If there was anything worse about New York than the job I had, it was the room I lived in—the only one of ten or twelve I looked at that I could hope to afford. I've never been very particular about where I sleep or eat, but this place was bad even by my standards.

It was on the third floor of an old hotel just off Columbus Circle. The furniture consisted of a single bed with a sagging mattress, a brown-stained sink, a hot plate, a wooden chair, and a small black-and-white television set on a rusty metal stand. The only window looked out to a dirty brick wall so close I could have touched it, if the window had opened. Twenty-five or thirty tenants on the floor shared a bathroom down the hall.

I did my laundry in that room, without soap, in water heated on the hot plate. I never had breakfast, except for an occasional glass of juice. My Nedick's lunch was the best meal of the day. Seven nights a week, my dinner consisted of spaghetti boiled in an empty juice can, topped with stewed tomatoes. Once, when I somehow lost a ten-dollar bill and couldn't come up with my rent on time, the hotel locked me out of my room. I spent a very long night in Grand Central Station and reported to work in the morning exhausted and even hungrier than usual. Luckily, a friend I'd made who worked in the stockroom of the toy department was able to lend me a few dollars; and by pawning my watch for a few dollars more, I managed to pay the rent.

•

I've never figured out whether what happened my first
night back in the room was coincidence or the result of a
very stupid robber's plan. I'd eaten my spaghetti dinner,
watched a western on the television (a show about a marshal with a trick gun that always made him faster than the
bad guys), and then attached the chain lock inside the door
and gone to bed, exhausted. That hotel was a noisy place,
but I fell immediately into a deep sleep.

I was awakened by a rattling sound. I tried to ignore it,
but it wouldn't go away. It must have been quite late
because that was the only sound I heard. When I finally
opened my eyes, I saw what was happening at once. My
door was open, showing a narrow shaft of yellow light from
the hall. A big hand in a black glove was fumbling with the
chain lock, trying to get it open. In that light from outside,
I saw it very clearly: a tight-fitting, shiny leather glove with
a thick, hairy wrist below it.

Looking back at the incident, my reaction seems cruel,
but at the time it was purely instinctive. Without a con-
scious thought, I threw the covers off and jumped to my
feet on the bed, and then I was flying through the air shoulder first, the way I'd delivered so many blocks on the football field. I hit the door so hard that, afterward, I was
surprised I hadn't crashed right through it. The man in the
glove screamed loudly enough to be heard out on Columbus Circle. The next sound I heard, after I'd taken my
weight off the door, was feet pounding heavily down the
hallway. I stood there against the door, heart pounding,
breathing hard, and in a while I checked the lock and went
back to bed. But I didn't sleep again that night. I lay there
wondering whether someone had found out I'd been

•

locked out of my room, and whether anybody could be dumb enough not to realize that a room locked from the inside had somebody in it. But it didn't really matter. All I knew for sure was that I had to get out of New York as soon as possible.

That was why I signed up to march in Macy's Thanksgiving Day parade. The pay would be twenty dollars, enough to get me somewhere else—and anywhere else would do.

This was at a time when westerns such as the one I'd seen the night I crushed the gloved hand were very popular on weekly television, and several cowboy stars were featured in the parade that year. (Besides them, all I remember vividly are Pilgrims in black suits, colorfully dressed clowns, and marching bands playing horrible music.)

I marched as an Indian. Inside the store, half an hour

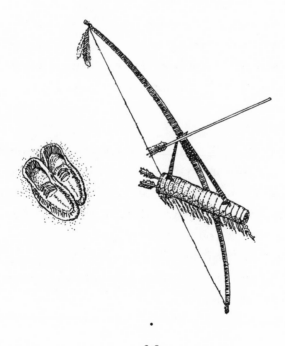

·

before the parade was scheduled to begin, I was suited up in imitation leather leggings, a fringed vest, moccasins a size or two small, and a tight elastic headband with two short, bedraggled feathers in it. Another bald man, this one in a gray suit and a bow tie, looked me over approvingly. (If I'd shaved my head as well as my beard, maybe they *would* have given me a decent job at Macy's.)

"You look positively excellent," he said, then handed me a cheap wooden bow and an arrow without a point to carry and told me that my place in the parade would be just behind the famous cowboys.

"And don't forget to wave," he added.

"At who?"

"Why, at everybody. Children. People watching the parade. It means a lot to spectators if you smile and wave at them as you're going by. You're one of our happy redmen after all!"

On my way out of the store, among crowds of Pilgrims, I ran into another young man in leggings, moccasins, a fringed vest, and a headband. His had a single feather in it.

"You know where you're going?" I asked him.

"Nope. You?"

"Not really."

"What the hell, then. We might as well go together, hey?" He had a heavy New York accent and a friendly smile, and we made our way slowly through the Pilgrims. "Nobody gave *me* any bow and arrow," he said, "and I'm in sports. Where do you work?"

"The shoe department."

"They never even give me a tommyhawk. Or two god-damn feathers, even."

·

"You want one of mine?"

"Naw!"

We introduced ourselves. His name was Carpenelli, and he'd been born and raised in Brooklyn, near Coney Island. He said he was sorry he'd let his boss pressure him into walking in the parade because he'd be missing the first hour or two of a four- or five-hour Thanksgiving dinner at home. "We got it all," he said. "All the antipasto. The pasta. Italian bread. Italian sausage. Italian steak. Italian veal. Italian turkey. Italian ice cream. Italian coffee. I got a family knows how to *eat!*"

Outside the store, we became two among hundreds of costumed marchers looking for our places. The day was cold for late November, with a solid gray overcast, a temperature down in the twenties, and a wind so strong down some of the streets that blowing grit stung my bare arms.

"They coulda maybe made us Eskimos," Carpenelli said. "Where *you* from?"

"Born in Buffalo. I grew up down in Pennsylvania. But I've been mostly out west lately. I'm heading west in a few days."

"Yeah? Jeez, I wish I could! Out west or down south, maybe. Maybe I'll do it someday. Florida. California. But my family, they been right around here in Brooklyn forever. Dozens. *Hundreds* of 'em. Aunts, uncles, cousins, nieces, nephews, the works. Another year or two, maybe then I'll do it. Take off, hit the damn road!" (It was something I heard from at least one-third of the people I talked to in New York: they claimed they wanted to leave town, but few sounded as if they'd ever do it.)

We finally found our place. There were eight or ten

·

other "Indians" there already, all of them dressed exactly as we were, two with bows and arrows and the rest of them empty-handed. We were to march in a group directly behind the four mounted cowboys. (Of the four, I recognized two; one who played the fearless marshal of a lawless western town and one who played the stupid deputy of another fearless marshal.)

One of the cowboys—the stupid deputy—walked his horse back to us just before the parade began. It was obviously a case of a celebrity's proving himself in public to be a real human being by briefly associating with nobodies.

"Cold enough for you hombres?" he said happily, smiling down from his elaborate silver-studded saddle.

"Hey, I watch you every week!" Carpenelli answered.

"Good, great!" the cowboy said.

"I liked that one where they shot that guy's hat right off his head—*blam! blam!*—and he never even blinked! That one where they shot off his hat and he kept right on eating his dinner!"

"That was a good 'un!" the cowboy said, and he turned his horse and walked it back to his place.

"You watch that program?" Carpenelli asked me. "The one he's on?"

"I've seen it a few times," I said.

Looking back at it now, all it seems is funny. My feet ached in the tight moccasins, I was numbed by the cold and wind, and it seemed to take hours for us to get from where we started to where we were allowed to quit.

I made no effort to meet any of my fellow "Indians" other than Carpenelli, and it was too cold to do much talking to him. I ignored the crowds lining the streets in front of the long rows of tall, drab buildings. Despite my instructions to smile and wave, I couldn't come close to making myself do it. (Carpenelli and the other tribe members followed orders.) Sometimes I glanced at a child, bundled up and looking as cold and miserable as I was, and I felt sorry for it. Whenever I looked at adults, most of whom appeared bored, the same thought repeated itself in my mind: *A lot of this state used to be Mohawk country, but you own everything now. Two hundred years ago it was different, and three hundred years ago it was really different, but now you've got it all.*

Just ahead, the cowboys smiled and waved their big white hats continuously, in all directions. They rode in circles, coming back at us—but never looking at us, not even the deputy—and then turning away again.

And their big, shiny horses seemed to crap continuously, too. The only explanation that occurred to me was that, because of the cold weather, the animals had been fed extra rations sometime not long before the parade began.

The horses pranced (could that have been a contributing factor?), the cowboys waved their hats and smiled, the tails of the horses lifted regularly, and the crap steamed in the cold air as we dodged and weaved our way through it.

At one point, Carpenelli said, "At home, my ma's haulin' in the platters, an' all I got here is horse shit!"

"I wish this arrow had a point," I told him.

"How come?"

"I'd use it."

"On what?"

"I'd shoot a cowboy in the ass."

•

·

"Naw!" he said. "Naw!"

He seemed genuinely shocked, and we didn't speak again.

The entire experience was ridiculous. It was humiliating. For weeks afterward, I felt ashamed every time I thought about it.

But the twenty dollars got me well out of town and headed west again.

·

3

. . .

Off the

Reservation

The only place in America where "real Indians" can live together in numbers is on the reservations. I had my first brief glimpse of reservation life not long after I left Pennsylvania with my parents, when my mother and I were traveling by Greyhound from Texas to California to join

.

my father, who thought he might have found a job. We were somewhere in an Arizona desert, and the back half of the bus was filled with Indians.

Late at night, four young men on the long seat at the very rear got up and insisted I go back where they'd been sitting and lie down.

"Let him sleep," one of them said to my mother. "Let the boy stretch out and lie down."

So I lay on the backseat; but instead of sleeping, I watched and listened.

The women were wrapped in colored blankets against the chill of the night, and the men wore long-sleeved shirts, many smoking orange-glowing cigarettes as they talked quietly and, sometimes, laughed together in the dark. Some of the men drank from bottles, and some of the women looked back at me from time to time and smiled. There was a strong odor of smoke and leather, and of bourbon, so I was reminded of Granddad Brant's barn.

In the early morning, when it wasn't quite light, the bus pulled to a slow stop at a little shack at a crossroads, and all the Indians filed off.

"Where do they live?" I asked my mother.

"On a reservation near here."

"It must be pretty nice."

"No," she said. "It isn't."

"I wish I lived there."

"No," she said. "You don't."

A few years later, I would learn how right she was.

In my travels I visited reservations in Montana, Ari-

·

zona, New Mexico, Oklahoma, Washington, Oregon, and California. Everything I saw there has been documented often, and more effectively than I can do it: the sub-standard housing, the unemployment, the depression, the violence, the alcoholism, and the suicides.

Few of the people on reservations really want to be there. The obvious problem, of course, is that escaping to a better life is often impossible and never easy. The year after I left Macy's and New York, I met two good young people in Oklahoma who tried.

I was hitchhiking from Louisiana to Colorado to see friends. Thanks to a few months of tolerable odd jobs, I had a little money saved. An artillery sergeant who was stationed at Fort Sill picked me up just outside Wichita Falls, Texas, where he'd been on pass, and drove me north to Lawton, which was obviously an army town.

The sergeant, a black man from South Carolina, a career soldier, told me about the Lawton whores as he drove. Aside from talking about the whores, he swore every few minutes, whenever a bug splattered against the windshield. He was a big man with a high voice and a heavy southern drawl that was nice to listen to, even when he swore.

"Some of the whores is pretty young," he said. "Mostly they work in the hotels. Man, on payday cats is lined up way around the block. But it ain't close to payday now, so now's the good time." We were driving along a two-lane road at dusk, and he smiled and tapped the steering wheel with his thick black fingers. "Me, I save up my money till all the other cats is broke," he said. "Hell, man, a week, ten days after payday, most of 'em is bummin' smokes already. You get any girl you want then—once you got one picked out

·

you want regular—and she ain't in any special hurry, either. Plenty whores in Lawton, but there ain't ever *enough* in any army town. I been all over. Korea. Germany. I'm goin' *back* overseas, too, soon's my tour's done here."

"You like it better overseas?"

"Hell, yes, I do."

"Did you fight in Korea?"

"Hell, no! I got there *after* that." Another bug hit the windshield. "They got the biggest son-of-a-bitchin' bugs I ever *seen* down here, man. Like *birds.*"

"Can you drop me off in the middle of town?"

"Anyplace you want. I'm goin' straight on up to Sill."

I had some money, I was young, and it wasn't close to payday; so in Lawton I found a whore. After three glasses of bad draft beer, a bartender told me where to go.

The adjective "dingy" might have been invented for this hotel: worn carpets, peeling paint, burnt-out light bulbs, water-stained ceilings, dust, cobwebs, dead bugs, the stale odors of rancid food. It was at least as bad as my room off Columbus Circle in New York.

At the end of a long hallway, I found her room: Number 503. That same number had been my street address as a child in Pennsylvania; and when I saw it on the door and remembered, it made me sad.

The room was much like the rest of the place: an old wooden rocking chair, a portable radio on a rickety night-stand, a naked light bulb hanging from a cord, faded wall-paper with birds in flight dimly visible on it, and, in the far corner, away from the shaded window, a double bed with rumpled gray sheets partly covered by an olive drab army blanket.

•

The girl wasn't lovely, not even very pretty. She was healthy, young, and frightened. Her long, dark hair was tied in a braid with a red ribbon. She wore a blue cotton blouse, faded jeans, and scuffed brown leather shoes. Her brown skin was immaculate, and her dark eyes shone. "Jerry sent you?" she asked. I was more than a foot taller than she was; so, staring straight ahead, she was looking at my chest.

"The bald guy at the bar on the corner," I said.

"That's him. That's Jerry."

When she stepped aside, I walked into the room, and she closed the door behind me. Then she walked toward the bed but stopped in the middle of the room, underneath the light bulb. "What you want?" she said.

I'd decided what I wanted the moment she opened the door. "Nothing," I told her.

"Then what the hell you here for?" Everything she said was in the same flat voice, conveying absolutely nothing.

I gave her the money—I don't remember how much it was, no more than ten dollars—and we talked for a while. It was awkward, and neither of us said much that first night. A lot of the awkwardness had to do with that room—not so much its shabbiness, but the knowledge both of us had of what she did there.

When I'd gone back three or four nights in a row, I finally talked her into leaving the hotel with me. (I never insulted her with money after the first night.)

One time we went to a cheap café and drank coffee and talked. After that we found a small park with benches near the edge of town. The park included a playground, but even on warm nights, there were never any children there.

·

Plenty of them must have been there during the day, though, because all the grass had been worn away by running, scuffling feet. The only time I ever got her to smile was when I pushed her on one of the playground swings. Pushing her that way was the only time I ever touched her, and I felt that her body was thin and frail.

She called herself Peg. She was nineteen years old and lived with a brother a year younger in a shack on a dirt road somewhere near the Wichita Mountains. Both parents had been dead for a long time—she barely remembered them—and their other brothers and sisters, all older, lived with an aunt on a reservation.

The brother's name was Charlie. He didn't like me much at first, I thought, because of the way I'd met his sister. But he must have known that I'd never been her customer, that I was nothing to her but a friend; and finally, after several visits to the shack, we became friends, too.

It was a good shack—clean, neat. There was a wood stove used for both heat and cooking, a wooden table with four chairs, and two small beds made up with clean sheets and blankets. Peg's bed, in a corner, had a heavy woolen blanket hung for privacy. They used old wooden crates stood on end against the walls as shelves for their food, cooking utensils, and clothes. A Coleman lantern hung from a wire over the table. Out back was an outhouse. Charlie's car, an old green two-door Ford, was usually parked behind it, near the rocky bank of a dry ravine.

I lived in a cheap motel at the outskirts of town, worked at a construction job, and hitchhiked out to the shack on weekends. Peg was sometimes there, and Charlie always was. He drove her back and forth to the hotel.

•

Before Charlie began to like me, all we did was talk. Once, just before sundown, we were sitting on rocks on the bank of the dry ravine. Peg was in town at the hotel.

"How much school did you go to?" I asked him.

"I graduated high school last year."

"Really?"

"Hell, yes, really."

"What about a job?"

•

"What about it?"

"Do you want one?"

"I don't want to work in town. I *can't.*"

"What do you want to do?"

He picked up a small stone and began tossing it back and forth from one brown hand to the other. "I don't know yet. I like to run."

"You mean race?"

"I was the best runner at school. The best distance runner around this part of the country."

He was nearly as tall as I, but a good twenty-five or thirty pounds lighter, with very long, slender, smooth-skinned legs that were burned a dark reddish brown from the sun. I never saw him wear anything but white cotton shorts, white T-shirts, and high-top canvas sneakers with a small round hole worn through each red-rubber sole. The shorts and T-shirts were always clean, but the worn sneakers were darkened and streaked with dirt and dust.

"Maybe you could run in college," I said.

"What for? I can run out here." He threw the stone down into the ravine, where it clattered against bedrock, and then he motioned toward the open country across the ravine with his hand. In the fading evening light the barren hills were softened, lovely. "Why should I go to a college? I don't want any job in some town. In some building. In some *room.*" He motioned toward the countryside again, toward the hills. "I can run anywhere I want out there."

High above us a hawk screamed, and we both looked up and saw it, soaring in sunlight.

"Red-tail," he said. "Last week I saw a bobcat. Last

•

month I killed a deer. I hunt with a bow. When you cut open their throats, it makes a whistling sound. It's the only part I don't like about it."

"How far can you run?"

"Ten, twenty, thirty miles."

"Really?"

"Hell, yes."

"How often do you do it?"

"Every day. This time of year, it's coolest in the early morning. There's plenty coyotes out there. Sometimes a bear. Early morning's best for coyotes. They hunt at night and lay up someplace high in the day."

"I like coyotes."

"Me, too!"

When he began to like me more, we ran together. There were many trails and dirt roads through the hills, and Charlie would run beside me on the flats, speed ahead on the uphills, and then, when I was coming down off a hill, he would turn and run back up to meet me. If I ran ten miles a morning, he ended up running at least fifteen.

Charlie had the naturally fluid grace of a born distance runner: the long, effortless stride, the easy arm-swing, the soft footfall, the slight forward lean of the upper body.

It was during our early-morning runs that he opened up and talked about what really mattered to him. I never really prodded him—or even questioned him, except in ways that I thought might help him get what he wanted off his mind.

"Do you know what county we're in?" he asked me one day.

"No."

"Comanche County. There's a little town south of Lawton named Geronimo. I have some friends there. Up north and east is a big lake called Lake O' the Cherokees. I went there once to fish. Why did they keep our names on so many things?"

He didn't wait for an answer. We were starting up a long, straight, steep dirt road through cottonwoods and willows, and he lengthened his stride and without apparent effort steadily widened the distance between us.

Another morning, later on, he talked about his sister.

"I hate what Peg does. She won't stop no matter what I say. I always tell her to stop, but she won't."

"She hasn't been doing it long, has she?"

"Six months. Seven. Only since we left the reservation. She thinks she can save her money and go to some college. She thinks she can learn enough about something and then go somewhere for a better life."

"She told me what she was saving for. Where does she want to go?"

"She doesn't even know. Somewhere far away. East or west, it doesn't matter to her."

"Maybe she can."

"She's smart."

"I know. It's easy to tell."

"But I hate what she does. It makes me sick." He spat to the side of the road. "But she's saving her money. She won't stop. How else can she make money?"

"I don't know," I said.

We were starting up a hill, but this time he stayed beside me.

·

"She wants to try to live a regular white kind of life," Charlie said. "I don't want to—I *can't*—but she does. Do you know the kind of men she sees?"

"I know about the army."

"It makes me goddamn sick!"

"She's not a bad person, though," I said. "It's easy to tell that too."

"I don't know what to do. I make arrowheads, and they sell them to the dumb tourists. I carve little wooden birds and animals. Sometimes I think I could take rich white men hunting and fishing for pay, but I don't know what to do, how to start doing it. I don't know what to *do*. Do you think she can save enough and do what she wants?"

"Maybe," I said.

But she couldn't.

She was murdered in Lawton after a payday. It happened in the early morning, just before dawn, when she was walking from the old hotel toward an all-night café to meet Charlie, who was waiting there to drive her back to their shack in his Ford. She was beaten to death and robbed on a side street, near a closed gas station; and only minutes after it happened, her body was found between two parked cars by three drunken GIs. The body was still warm, and they thought she might be alive, but she wasn't. Nobody was ever arrested for it.

A few days later, in the early morning out in the Wichita Mountains, Charlie drove the Ford into a tree. The car had been traveling at high speed—top speed, probably—and

·

afterward the police who investigated claimed he'd been drunk and that the death was accidental. But I doubt if Charlie had anything to drink, and I'm sure nobody cared enough to find out for sure one way or another, because a lot of Indians drove drunk and killed themselves, and they must have figured they could just let it go at that.

4

. . .

Ancient

Pursuit

Out in the barn, sipping his whiskey, Granddad Brant told me about the way he killed a deer each winter.

In the early morning, after a fresh snow—but no more than two or three inches—he hiked the open country beyond the trout stream until he found the tracks of a good-

.

sized buck. Carrying the single-shot .22 rifle slung across his shoulder and a little food but no water—he could use the snow for that—he set out after the buck at a fast, steady walk. When he was lucky, he would find where the buck had bedded down for the day within an hour or two, and if the cover wasn't too thick he could spook it from its hiding place and watch as it bounded away. Then he would set out after it again, tracking at the same fast walk.

The winter days were short, but sometimes they were long enough. He would track the deer through the morning and afternoon, usually forcing it from cover two or three more times before it became too exhausted to stay ahead of him.

"Deer run fast," he explained. "You've seen them do it. But they can't keep going as long as a man can. The Mohawks used to run them down sometimes. Sometimes they did it the same way I do."

After six, eight, or even ten hours of the fast, relentless walking, he would finally come up on the exhausted buck, head hanging, hot breath steaming in the winter air.

"I worked hard enough to have a right to kill it," he explained.

And he did kill it, with a close-range round from the .22 placed carefully through the small brain.

An irrigation ditch runs for miles along the southeastern slopes of the glacial foothills not far from our home. The ditch is fed by a large reservoir a few miles south of us, and the water is used by farmers, ranchers, and orchardists a few miles farther north. The land in between, where I was

·

headed, belonged to cattle ranchers years ago, but these ranches finally failed, mostly because of overgrazing. Now the fields are star thistle and sparse knee-high range grass, with dense little willow thickets every quarter- or half-mile, wherever there are springs.

There are still some pheasants to be found, if you have a decent dog. Now, in summer—and this was an unusually dry one—deer would come down the slopes for water. There really isn't any other water in a drought year. Often a deer will bed in one of the willow thickets near the ditch. I was looking for a chance to run deer as Mohawks used to, to pay respect to both John and Joseph Brant, to challenge myself, to draw close to the life of the land. What Granddad Brant explained to me is quite true: deer are born for sprinting, for short bursts of speed, so sometimes it's possible, in open country with luck and sufficient endurance, to run one down.

I parked at the end of a gravel road a couple of hundred yards below the irrigation ditch. It was very hot, four o'clock, a good day to sweat hard and to learn what kind of shape I was in.

From where I parked, a barely visible trail led through the dry grass up a long hillside to the bank of the irrigation ditch. My plan was to work south, checking every willow thicket within a hundred yards of water along the way, looking for a bedded deer.

By the time I reached the water, I was sweating. Later, I knew, if I found my deer, I might drink that muddy water thirstily.

My legs felt good, and I started south at something just under the pace of an aging distance man.

·

Along both banks of the ditch, the grass was thick and lush from seepage. In my first quarter-mile I flushed three pheasants: two cocks and a hen. Then a flock of at least eight birds exploded from the grass beside me, the cocks crowing loudly as they whirred away and then glided down the hill to disappear into the high brown grass.

It was easy running beside the ditch. The county works on the irrigation system periodically throughout the year, and their Jeeps and four-wheel-drive pickups keep the ground packed smooth and hard—and it was cooler by the water, by at least five degrees.

I've run for so long that once I get warm and loosen up, it becomes automatic. There are obvious physical limitations, but I'm seldom aware of them in the beginning. I'm aware of earth, wind, and movement, as if I'm being carried along by some outside power.

The first of the willow thickets was about half a mile from where I started, fifty yards up a hillside from the ditch. I spotted a stone, scooped it up without stopping, threw it into the thicket, and yelled loudly as it clattered against the willow branches. One hen pheasant flushed, and nothing more.

A quarter-mile farther on was the first of the thickets with real potential. Just twenty yards downhill from the ditch, it was thickly lush and green. The thicket itself, about half the size of a basketball court, was swampy enough on the downhill side so that snipe held there in the fall.

A large stone in each hand, I jogged down to it through the star thistle. Breathing deeply, I stood in warm shade on the uphill side. The thicket was even denser than I remem-

·

bered—much too thick to see into. I tossed the first stone, shook the slender trunk of a willow, and yelled. There was a heavy thrashing deep within the willows, then a whirring of wings, and a covey of thirty or forty valley quail burst out in all directions. A pheasant came behind them—another crowing cock this time—and then the deer. I heard the deer before I saw it, crashing out the bottom end. I circled around the top to avoid the swampy area and saw that it was a young buck.

I dropped the second stone and started after him. He had a forty- or fifty-yard head start, going south, parallel with the ditch above us, and his head was turned to watch me as he picked up speed. I held my pace and angled back to the firmer footing along the ditch.

The springy, almost jumping gait of the deer was beautiful to see. His raised tail and rump were startlingly white

in the dusty heat, and small clouds of powdery dust rose like smoke behind him.

I kept my pace. I'd covered better than a quarter-mile by now without tiring. He stayed below the ditch, heading, as I'd hoped he would, for the next thicket along the way.

By then I was sweating hard, but my legs were fine. As he entered the thicket, I was little more than three hundred yards behind. I could see him there in the willows, see the white rump; and then even closer, the turned head with its glassy brown eyes staring back at me in fright. A hundred yards away, I yelled, and this time he broke out from the top end, raced straight up the hill, and cleared the irrigation ditch with one long, graceful bound. It was lucky for me, because by coming up the hill, he had actually shortened the distance between us.

Once across the ditch, he picked up speed again. The next mile or two, I knew, would be the hardest; but after that his fright would actually work to my advantage.

He started up the slope on the other side of the ditch, stopped, turned again to look, then headed straight for the nearest thicket. I had to increase my pace. My legs hadn't begun to tire, but my breath was coming hard now, and my side ached slightly. Two hundred yards above me, and twice that far ahead, the buck reached the sparse thicket near the long-deserted ranch house with the tangled blackberry vines and the rusted-out Model T in the yard.

As I approached, I saw his chest heaving, his muscular rear legs trembling, as he watched me cross the ditch and start directly toward him.

The cool water felt good on my feet, and I cupped some into my face and rinsed out my mouth with a palmful.

•

Past the ranch house was a brushy draw that reached up a mile east, then a half-mile north to another old homestead site. It appeared that the buck would jump the draw; but he hesitated, then made a wheeling turn and started up along it. I turned, too, and angled up toward him. Near the homestead site was a long-neglected apple orchard, an acre of trees planted decades ago. The old, gnarled trees bore fruit, and I knew the buck would head there now if that was where he had been feeding.

If he followed the draw to the orchard, he'd cover the whole mile and a half. From where I was I could cut the distance nearly in half by heading straight up over a hill and down the other side to the orchard.

I decided to try it. If the buck changed course—if he crossed the draw and headed south—I still might catch him. If he was on a familiar route to the orchard, I knew I would.

My legs were heavy now, and my side ached badly—but all that is a challenge when you love to run. Going up the long hill, I would pick out a conspicuous stone or a dense patch of star thistle a hundred or so yards away, tell myself to hold the pace until I reached it, and then, when I was finally there, I'd find another object farther on. Downhill to my right, to the south, I could see the buck the whole way.

Already I could see that he had slowed. His gait wasn't nearly so springy now, and he didn't hold his head so high. There was no doubt now that he was heading for the orchard.

I reached the crest of the hill without having had to slow my pace, and it was relatively easy going down the other side, using different muscles. In fact, the hard part going down was slowing so as not to reach the orchard ahead of the buck. If that happened, he might not stay on my side of the draw.

It all went well. Twenty minutes later, the buck was exhausted. The orchard made it relatively easy for me. He was determined not to leave it. Evidently he had fed on the apples often, and somehow that must have made him feel secure there. Each time I scared him out of the trees, he would make a wide, nervous arc and finally enter them again.

By the time he stood trembling, too exhausted to move, I was refreshed and rested. I had run around the orchard a number of times, keeping close in to the trees, while he—in his wider circles—had covered miles.

Now he stood about twenty yards out from the orchard's west edge, facing west and looking back at me. Outside the trees myself, I slowed to a walk. I was only ten yards away from him. He took a tentative step, but his head sank. He could go no farther, and I stopped where I was and talked to him soothingly.

Flies circled his back, but he was trembling so severely that they couldn't light. When the trembling finally eased, the flies alighted.

I walked slowly up and touched his warm, sweaty flank. He started away, jerkily and graceless for the first few steps, then with increasing strength and confidence, and all the way his head was turned to watch me.

A hundred yards away, he stopped. His eyes left mine, and now he seemed to study the country. Then he circled back to the draw, but this time he crossed it. He headed south and was out of sight in less than a minute.

•

•

I could still feel his lovely wildness on my hand where I had touched him.

All of the green apples had been eaten from the lowest branches of the trees. I had to jump to get one. The fruit was hard, sour, and delicious. When I finished the apple, I ran back to the car.

•

5

. . .

The Day

before

Thanksgiving

I had taken my fly rod south to California's Klamath River. It was early on the Wednesday morning before Thanksgiving.

On this cloudless fall morning, the waters of the stream were much warmer than the air, a climatic condition which

.

created a surreal effect, something like a romanticist's visu-
alization of heaven. A thin layer of undulating white mist
hung closely over the river's surface, so dense that the water
was barely visible beneath it, even as I waded.

It was very cold—at least ten degrees below freezing—
as I made my way slowly upstream toward the head of a
long riffle. Ice would form in the rod guides today. In the
dawn light, the local mallards had begun their downstream
flight toward a morning feeding, coming in pairs and small
flocks every minute or two. With duck season well under
way, undoubtedly these birds had been hunted and shot at,
but they ignored me as their rapid wing beats carried them
along in easy shotgun range, so close that I could hear the
hissing rush of their passage. Hidden as I was from the
waist down by the layer of mist, perhaps they didn't recog-
nize me as a man.

Just twenty yards up the ridge of slippery, algae-covered
rocks that I was wading, and close against the edge of the
ridge, was a deep slot protected at its top end by a cluster of
boulders. I couldn't see the place, but I knew its exact location from many previous trips, and from where my feet told
me I was as I carefully felt my way along.

My first short cast was accurate, and the steelhead took
the fly the instant it touched water. The line tightened hard
at the strike, and the fish jumped, glowing pinkish silver,
appearing phosphorescent in the early light as it rose above
that white mist, hung there for a split second, then fell back
tail first with a loud splat before it ran downstream, hard.

I played it clumsily with numbed hands, but it was
hooked securely, and a few minutes later I landed a bright
five-pound female. We always release the females to spawn;

•

and as I lowered this one back into the river, the water felt as warm as a bath in the chill morning air.

If that first fish had been a male, I would have killed it and headed home, back over Siskiyou Pass to Oregon. Instead, I worked down the long riffle, first stripping a yard of line between casts until I had about sixty feet out, then taking one long step downstream between my casts, occasionally soaking the rod in the river to melt the ice from the guides. As far as I could see in either direction, I had the river to myself, and no cars or log trucks passed on the road behind me.

Fifteen or twenty minutes later, the second steelhead of the morning struck. I was just over halfway down the riffle, the fly, a Number Six Skunk, hanging straight below me, no more than an inch beneath the surface on my floating line.

The mist had evaporated, and this fish—probably it had followed the fly in from midstream—slashed across the

surface, showing both its dorsal fin and tail, and, without jumping, it was off on a long, hard downstream run, angling back toward the middle of the river. Fifty or sixty yards down, it held out there in a foam-flecked eddy behind a huge smooth-topped boulder that broke the river's surface by an inch or two. Holding the rod high, I reeled to tighten the line, then put on all the pressure the six-pound leader could take. I couldn't budge the fish; and since it hadn't jumped at the strike and was holding that way, solid and immovable, I was certain it was a male.

I waded down, reeling to keep the line tight. Stumbling over rocks, nearly falling twice, I went all the way down to a little island thick with willows near the tail of the riffle. Below the fish now, with my feet on solid ground, I drew him out of the eddy. When he hit the current he made another downstream run, but this only brought him nearer to me. I tightened the line again, then patiently worked him in.

It was another five-pounder, a dark male, and I killed it and cleaned it, leaving the entrails and strips of milt in the willows. Something that could use them would find them there. As I washed my hands and knife in the stream, a gray heron flew silently over my head and settled on a dead fir tree fifty yards upstream. The ducks were no longer flying, and the first shafts of morning sunlight hit the red-orange leaves of streamside maple trees.

When I carried the fish up to the car, the Indian children were there, a boy of about eleven, a girl of nine. They waited on the Klamath River Road for their school bus every weekday morning, so I had run into them often over the years. Their small, dilapidated cabin was set a hundred

·

yards back in a deep, narrow draw across the road. The only signs of life I'd ever seen from the place were the two children and the blue-gray smoke that curled from the stovepipe chimney on cold mornings like this one.

I smiled at them and said hello, as I always did; and, as always, neither of them answered. Dressed in patched jeans that were inches too short, high-topped canvas sneakers, and faded poplin jackets, their cheeks and the knuckles of their gloveless hands red with cold, they stared at my fish. The boy wore a brown woolen cap pulled low over his head, and carried a schoolbook with George Washington's picture on the cover.

"Don't you two ever go fishing?" I asked them. I didn't expect an answer, but I wanted to say something as I opened the back of the car, disjointed my fly rod, and prepared to leave. "It's a pretty good year for them," I continued. "Not what it used to be, but pretty good. Right out there where you see me fishing is as good as any spot on the whole upper river, and you live right next to it. You'd still have time after school. They'll take worms or just about anything."

The whole time I spoke, they stood there six feet away on the gravel shoulder of the road, staring at the steelhead, which I had laid out on an old towel in the car.

"Do you want it?" I finally asked, picking it up, holding it out toward them, my cold index finger through the gill. "I can always get another one, I think."

The boy looked into my eyes for a second or two, and my impression was that he very nearly smiled. Instead, he looked down at the ground and took three short steps forward, reached out and took the fish, and then both of them turned and sprinted across the road and up the steep dirt

·

path toward the cabin. I could hear the scuffing of their sneakers on the hard-packed earth, and see their puffs of breath in the cold morning air as they ran. About halfway up the path, the boy dropped the fish. The girl quickly scooped it up and they kept on running.

"You were born way too late," I said aloud to myself. "Even later than I was."

I was fairly sure the family could use the steelhead and hoped they would enjoy it, but I had no idea how the adults inside might react to such a gift. I assumed, for no very good reason, that they were Hoopas who didn't want to live on their reservation land farther downstream. I'd seen that reservation—the unemployment and the drinking—and it wasn't a place for children to grow. The father might have a job somewhere in Hornbrook or Yreka—an old pickup truck was parked outside—or they might subsist off the

·

land somehow. There were plenty of deer in this country, but I couldn't see a garden from the road. I was sure they'd seen me fishing from the cabin; and I knew that, had they wanted to meet me, they would have come outside before this to say hello. Somehow they made me remember Peg and Charlie in Oklahoma, long ago. I left in a hurry and drove downstream.

It took me until noon to catch another steelhead. Wanting a male to kill, it was next to inevitable that I would land a female at each of the next two spots I fished, the second of them a nice six-pounder. Then, on my way back up from that fish, I found the artifacts of my two widely separated cultures in plain view, not six inches apart in the dusty earth in the shade of a blackberry bush: a broken-pointed obsidian arrowhead and a crushed aluminum 7UP can. I left the arrowhead where it lay—why disturb it?—and took the can back to the car to dispose of it later.

After that I fished four more spots without a rise, then finally hooked and landed my male at a place I hadn't tried in several years. It was a long, rocky riffle, fairly shallow, that deepened and slowed abruptly at its bottom end, where it entered a pool. This four-pounder was holding near the far bank, just up over the lip of the riffle, and when I landed it I saw how lucky I had been. He was hooked by a fragile layer of nearly transparent skin on his upper lip.

Walking back to the car through thick tangles of black-berry bushes and a stand of pines, I was sweating in my waders. The temperature had climbed to at least fifty degrees, with the sky a cloudless washed-out blue: Indian summer weather at its best.

I started home. Not far upstream from where I'd landed

·

my fish were the scars created by hydraulic placer miners more than a century ago. I remember that Joaquin Miller had described the devastation left by Klamath River miners in *Life Amongst the Modocs,* published in 1873. Entire sections of bank have been hacked and gouged away and remain as the miners left them, in huge ugly piles like the slag heaps that disfigured the industrial towns of Pennsylvania when I was a boy.

The Klamath has been exploited for its timber and its fish as well as its gold, and the most recent fortune seekers to move into the area are marijuana farmers. The previous summer I'd been fishing the south bank of the upper Klamath for trout. At lunchtime I took a break and hiked up a steep draw and across a ridge, then followed a small creek down a gentle slope in the pleasant shade of fir trees. Rounding a bend in the creek, I was suddenly confronted by one of the wildest-looking gentlemen I've ever seen: tangles of foot-long hair, a thick red beard, a mustache like Yosemite Sam's, tattered jeans, and a T-shirt that looked as though it might last have been laundered in the mid-1960s. To complete the image, there were two big revolvers strapped to his hips, their dark metal gleaming beneath a film of oil. A hundred years earlier, similar men became the "Indian hunters" who helped eradicate the local tribes, winning status as heroes for their efforts.

His right hand resting on the butt of one of the guns, this specimen told me to turn around and get back to wherever I'd come from. I did. Such confrontations aren't uncommon these days. In many northwest counties, marijuana is said to be the major cash crop, now that most of the old-growth trees have been stripped away.

·

I passed the Indian family's cabin, which was still in shade, a thin trail of blue smoke curling from its chimney. Perhaps they were Modocs and not Hoopas. In any case, it was clear they weren't enjoying much of their country's wealth.

•

On the drive back home over the mountains, I tried to decide where to hunt mountain quail in the afternoon, and then I remembered Granddad Brant, as I often do. I thought of the day he had me wade into the creek to get close to the feeding trout. That experience with patience had carried me over many years and across a continent.

Before I ever hunted mountain quail, I hiked through their country without a gun and watched and learned. Once, late on a summer evening—an evening much like the one when I had seen the trout—I sat motionless, my back against the rough-barked trunk of an old white oak, in a grassy clearing where I had seen a covey feeding late on previous days. The quail arrived on schedule, fourteen of them walking stiff-legged and erect in single file down a brushy hillside in the fading light, but they stopped abruptly when the lead bird saw me, and they never came into the clearing. Instead, they fed into the buck brush up the hillside.

But I came back every evening for five straight days to sit with my back against the same oak, wearing the same clothes. Each evening the covey of mountain quail, slowly growing accustomed to my being there, came a little closer. By the last evening, they fed all around me, unconcerned and clucking softly from all sides. Warm wind moved through the tops of the tallest ponderosa pines on the hillside. Steller's jays scolded from a quarter-mile or more away, and, from somewhere closer, mourning doves called softly.

I'd been there a long time when one quail, a full-grown adult—a male, I was sure, because of its size—brushed his white- and chestnut-striped flank against the sole of my boot as he walked past, pecking seeds from the dusty earth. Slowly, without any indication he knew I was there, the

·

quail fed on the seeds until he was several yards away. Still in my field of vision, he turned and retraced his steps back in my direction. He brushed against my foot a second time, and then fed slowly off the other way until he was out of sight.

No hunting success—not the most difficult shot or the steepest climb—has ever made me feel better than that momentary contact did. That light, barely perceptible brushing of a bird's flank against my boot was the communion at the heart of it all—a direct connection with wild, unspoiled nature, and with my past.

To keep what I'd felt as long as possible, I stayed motionless against the oak tree trunk until it was nearly dark. The wind had died and a pale crescent moon had risen over the dark outlines of eastern hills. When all the quail had disappeared back up the hillside to wherever the covey roosted, I finally got to my feet and headed home. Granddad Brant was with me.

Back home from fishing, I wrapped the steelhead in foil and put it into the refrigerator. Hilde was out, but on the kitchen counter were two freshly baked blackberry pies, still warm, delicious smelling, made with fruit we had picked in early September. Southern Oregon's Bear Creek Valley is a fertile place. Besides the blackberries, summer and fall had supplied us with cherries, raspberries, strawberries, snow peas, corn, tomatoes, squash, peaches, pears, apples, and plums.

After a quick lunch, I changed from fishing into hunting clothes. When I walked out the back door to get Dog

·

from his pen, he was pawing at the gate and whining, well aware of what we were about to do.

It was just past two o'clock when I parked at the end of a rutted dirt road five miles south of town. Gun over my shoulder, vest weighted down with shells, I started up a long, steep hill in sunlight. I let Dog run out ahead at will in the beginning, to work off at least part of his energy.

I was already sweating by the time I reached the top of the long hill. Dog had disappeared over the crest ahead of me. When I came over, I saw him sniffing with interest toward a patch of manzanita. Although I'd never seen a mountain quail within half a mile of this place, I jammed shells into the chambers and trotted up behind him, ready for birds to flush.

It was a dead fawn, born in the spring. The yellow-brown animal lay stiffly on its side in brown grass, a bullet hole visible high on its chest. It was a doe, and the hind-quarters had been cleanly carved away. It was clearly the work of a deer hunter unable to find a buck.

"Leave it!" I said to Dog. "Come on, let's go!"

We started down the long hill, through the oaks that were nearly bare now, and mountain mahogany and manzanita, toward a steep valley with a good creek cutting through it from steep cliffs a few miles to the northeast.

When we hit the creek, I called to Dog, "Close! Stay close!" Then we started up the long draw in the pleasant shade of ponderosa pines.

I was fairly hopeful we would find birds somewhere in the area, possibly in cover near the creek at this time of day, or as likely scattered up the hillsides to feed on weed seeds and fallen acorns. Half a mile along, near a willow thicket,

Dog hit his first scent, his nose to the ground and tail wagging hard. There were no quail now, but it was clear that they had been there, and not long ago.

Another half mile up the draw was a long-abandoned log cabin. It was usually beyond the cabin, in steeper country, that we found large coveys in the afternoons and evenings. Along the way today we saw a porcupine and a big jackrabbit. After several minor quillings as a puppy (none nearly so bad as what had happened to Pat at Granddad Brant's) Dog was smart enough to make a wide detour around the porcupine, but he started after the rabbit—it burst from a manzanita patch on the creek bank—and I had to whistle and then scold him back to heel.

Moments after I turned him loose to hunt again, about sixty yards beyond the cabin, he hit fresh scent. Then I heard the quail rustling nervously through dead leaves within the willows. I ran hard and was halfway there when the birds began to flush. They streamed out the top end of the willows, three or four of them, then six more, then ten or a dozen, all of them just out of range, all of them flying up the draw, low over the creek, curving through oak trees, the whir of their powerful wings loud and exciting as always in the quiet afternoon.

Dog crashed into the willows, whining and yelping now, pawing his way through the branches. Then two stragglers flushed out the top end. They went the same route the earlier birds had taken, and I was ready. Flying low and straight away at eye level, they were as easy as shots at mountain quail can be.

Proud, clearly delighted with the way things had turned out, Dog made the retrieves. I laid the gun carefully in the

•

grass and held the lovely birds to look at them, one in each hand.

"Good dog!" I said. "Good boy!"

When I'd field-dressed the quail and reloaded, we started up the draw after the rest of the covey.

I thought it would be fairly easy, but we chased them for nearly two hours. I climbed, crawled, slipped, stumbled, and sprinted after them. When I kept dog close, within twenty or thirty yards, the birds ran out ahead of us. When I turned him loose to chase them, they flushed far out of range. I rarely saw them, but I heard the whirring wings and Dog's yelps of frustration as, time after time, they sailed away from us, farther up the mountainside.

Finally, with no more than fifteen or twenty minutes of legal hunting time left in the day, we pinned them down. We were so far up the mountain now that the cabin was little more than a speck in the clearing far below us. A red-tailed hawk turned in a wide circle below us, out over the cabin. The timber had thinned, and the stunted brush was patchy here.

Legs aching, boots heavy, soaked with sweat despite the rapidly cooling evening, I jogged along a narrow, rocky gully where one of several small spring-fed creeks comes out of the cliffs. At the top end of the gully, which ran into the base of a cliff, was another little willow patch. There was no other cover near it, so the covey had to be there. Because it was a dead end, when they flushed it would have to be down the gully, directly over my head.

This time they came out in twos and threes, about twenty yards up when they passed directly over me, dark, hurtling silhouettes against the clear evening sky. I picked a

·

bird from the first bunch and hit it cleanly, the spreading puff of feathers showing against the sky after it dropped. I heard the lifeless thud against dry earth when it hit ground somewhere behind me.

I missed the first bird in the next bunch out—I'd been behind it, I knew—and then quickly jammed more shells into the chambers. The quail kept coming. A single bird flew out higher than the others, thirty yards up. I swung from behind it, saw the bird at the end of the barrel, pulled the trigger just as the barrel moved smoothly past, and kept on swinging after the shot. This one, traveling higher and faster than the others, dropped farther down the mountainside than the first one had.

Dog circled the little thicket, yelping loudly. Five or six more birds flushed after I had killed my second one, and I watched them fly.

"Come on, Dog! Dead bird! Look around!"

He found both birds where they had fallen. I field-dressed them and then we started home, the four quail making a pleasant weight in my game pouch.

On the way back down the mountain, both Dog and I drank several times from the creek. A flock of Canada geese passed over in a perfect **V**, headed south, probably toward the Sacramento Valley. It was dark long before we reached the car. I was exhausted, and as cold now as I had been in the morning mist on the Klamath. I had cut my left arm on a tree branch and sprained my right ankle slightly. Dog had done something to his left hind leg, and he was limping some, too.

Heading home, thinking about it, I couldn't quite decide how much I had enjoyed that long, lovely, complicated Wednesday. The hunting and fishing had certainly been good enough. There was an excellent meal to look forward to. We would bake the steelhead and roast the quail. With them would be sautéed snow peas, baked squash, corn bread with plum preserves, applesauce, the blackberry pies, and a white wine made by a friend.

But, as usual, much of what I had seen and experienced and thought about through the day confused things: the Indian family, the mining scars, the pot farmer, the hamstrung fawn.

I've known for a long time that fish and game are killed illegally for no good reason, that the land is cynically ravaged for profit, that people are, too. I engage in my ancient pursuits and love them, but I was born at least two centuries

·

late. It struck me again that the broken arrowhead and the relatively indestructible 7UP can were appropriate symbols of my dilemma.

And I realized that because Dog knew nothing of any of this, he was the fortunate one. Every day he hunted was a good one, and there were never any serious complications.

"You had a fine time for sure, didn't you?" I asked him.

Sprawled out on the rubber mat on the floor beside me, he stretched all four legs out straight and sighed in contentment.

"Lucky Dog," I said, and I truly meant it.

6

. . .

Uncontaminated

Man

On the warm evening of August 29, 1911, near Oroville,
California, an exhausted, frightened, and nearly starved
Yahi Indian who came to be known as Ishi—"Man"—
appeared mysteriously at the corral of a slaughterhouse.

.

About fifty years old, he wore only a tattered scrap of covered wagon canvas over his shoulders. He was discovered by butchers and soon driven by the sheriff to the county jail in Oroville, where he was locked in a cell for the insane. When word got out, as it quickly did, people came from great distances to see the captured man. The last wild Indian in North America, the last living member of his tribe, Ishi had emerged from the rugged canyon country east of Red Bluff. A few days later, on September 4, he was on his way to the San Francisco Bay area, where he would spend the last four-and-a-half years of his life under the care and study of University of California anthropologists, principally Alfred Kroeber, who called Ishi "the most uncivilized and uncontaminated man in the world today."

Ishi in Two Worlds, the well-known biography by Kroeber's widow Theodora, reports that virtually everyone who met Ishi was impressed with his dignity and kindness, which is quite surprising considering the fact that he and his people had long been hunted for bounties by local whites at the going rate of fifty cents per scalp.

I don't remember exactly when I learned of Ishi's story, but it was in the early 1960s, not long after Kroeber's book was published by the University of California. I do know that from the very start, I wanted to visit the country Ishi had come from, to see and feel the place and better imagine his life. Uncivilized and uncontaminated, Ishi was the last individual to experience the true wildness that, at the time of Columbus, was taken for granted by at least ten million North American Indians.

·

My father was a boy when Ishi appeared at the northern California slaughterhouse, and Granddad Brant was a middle-aged man. On August 29, 1981, seventy years to the very day after Ishi's capture, I finally traveled into the Yahi country with my son. The area is still wild and remote, with a lot of private land to go through before you can reach it, but our friend—call him Red Hawk—knew the right people and knew the way.

So it was that late in the warm afternoon Red Hawk, Pete, and I were grinding and bouncing along the extremely rough, barely discernible old Lassen Trail in a thirty-year-old jeep. All of us sat in front, our fly rods and backpacks wedged into the seat behind us, and with each mile that Red Hawk drove the hills grew steeper, the draws rockier, the dust thicker.

"At least the old thing's still running, even if it doesn't have springs," I said.

"Just so the engine doesn't die," Red Hawk answered, almost screaming to be heard above its vibrating whine. "If it does, we probably won't get it started again for an hour. Sometimes the brakes go out, too. And gas leaks onto the manifold these days. I don't know that much about it, but it seems possible the engine could catch fire that way. See the deer?"

I saw them—four tawny does beneath an oak on a hillside—and I was willing to change the subject, too. "They're almost tame," I said. "They must not see many people out here."

"None at all," Pete said. "They don't see any, do they?"

"Not many whites have ever been back here," Red Hawk agreed.

.

We took the jeep as far as it could go, parked it a few yards off the trail, and then carried our packs and rods a long way down a steep canyon wall. We could hear the sound of moving water—that lovely muted roar—long before we reached Mill Creek.

"I want trout for dinner," Red Hawk said. "I hope we make it in time."

It was close. When we hit level ground at last—which felt strange, like land to a sailor—and fought our way through some brush to the sandy beach that would be our campsite, it was dark enough so that bats were swooping and darting for insects over the stream.

We threw down our packs and rigged our rods in a hurry. It had been a while since I'd last used my trout gear, and I knew I should tie on a new leader tippet, but it was too dark. I had difficulty simply threading the leader through the rod guides and tying on a large wet fly—a maribou muddler—with a turle knot.

If I'd been thinking, I would have realized that it was enough to break off the bottom sections of the tapered leader and tie the fly to ten- or even twelve-pound test, because the trout wouldn't see the heavy line in the dark water. But I was too happy to think; and what I should have done didn't occur to me until, on my third or fourth short cast to the head of the campsite pool—a long, smooth stretch below a waterfall at a bend in the creek—I hooked a fish that felt as heavy as a salmon.

It acted like a salmon, too. Pete, who had been a little slower rigging up, was on the bank behind me when the fish struck. "Bring it in," he said. "That's dinner."

·

"I can't bring it in," I said. "It's huge."

This native trout was strong and running deep, taking a lot of line off the reel in a hurry. I had thought quickly enough to loosen the drag, and the fish finally stopped and held at the tail of the pool, twenty yards below us. It took several minutes to work it slowly and carefully to within ten feet of the bank; but just when I thought it was ready to let me lead it all the way in, it turned and made another downstream run. This time I followed partway and finally eased it into shallow water, up near the surface.

"Look at it!" Pete said.

"I'll never land it—not on this leader," I answered.

But, with Pete's help, I did. We cornered the rainbow in a foot of water over sand, scooped it up, and tossed it, thrashing, up onto the stony bank. It was quite a trout. We didn't measure or weigh it, but it was easily large enough to satisfy the three of us for dinner.

When I cleaned it, I saw that the stomach was packed with large grasshoppers. I washed it out, careful to scrape the blood from the backbone, wrapped it in foil, and broiled it in glowing embers at the edge of our fire. Few people have eaten wild trout killed directly out of the water and cleaned and cooked immediately, so few people have any idea how trout should really taste. There were fresh ripe Oregon peaches and a bottle of white wine chilled from the stream to go with it.

After dinner we talked for a couple of hours, about Ishi and the Yahis who had camped at this very spot before us.

"They had all the acorns they could use from these oaks," Red Hawk said. "Tomorrow you'll see big grinding

·

bowls in the caves. This looks like pretty barren country, but the Yahis had over a hundred plants they used for food and medicine back here."

"Do the salmon make it up here anymore?" Pete asked.

"Maybe a few. Probably none. Ishi used to spear them, right out there where you caught that trout. The last steelhead I saw was a couple of years ago. They drain Mill Creek nearly dry for irrigation down near the valley, for the farms and orchards. So all we have left up here now are the native trout. The migrating fish can't make it. But at least it's still wild country. There's plenty of caves no whites have ever been in. A friend of mine found one once with two human skeletons in it. He couldn't tell whether they were whites or Indians. He couldn't ever find the cave again, either, after that first time. The entrances are overgrown with brush most of the time. I found a quiver of arrows in a cave once, almost like new. Plenty of bowls and points. You'll see."

We also talked about the next day's fishing. It was the time of year for big green grasshoppers in the canyon, so we knew we would do best fishing our largest grasshopper imitations over the deepest pools. Before we turned in, Red Hawk told us of some recent encounters with local wildlife not far from our campsite—wild pigs, rattlesnakes, a resident cougar.

I awakened only once during the night, at about two or three A.M., and for a few minutes I lay on my back and watched the billions of stars in the slice of black sky visible between the canyon walls that towered above us. Somewhere I had read that there are more stars and planets than there are grains of sand on earth, and that everything we have on earth is duplicated somewhere else in the universe.

•

On a world out there somewhere, I hoped there were unspoiled streams with healthy runs of salmon and steelhead in them. In such an immensity, it seamed not just possible but likely—and perhaps if there was such a stream, a man was camped on a beach with his son and a friend under the light of a moon or two.

We explored and fished all through the next day. Red Hawk hiked downstream from camp, and Pete and I went upstream. Every time we rounded a bend, I found myself instinctively expecting to see people. All we saw, though, were hawks and herons, quail and deer, so we were casting flies to trout that hadn't been fished for in months or years, if ever. We used grasshopper imitations that came fairly close to matching the hoppers that were thick along the brushy banks, though any fly of roughly the right size probably would have worked as well.

Pete and I took turns at the pools as they came, also covering the likeliest-looking pocket water between pools, hooking and releasing trout to eighteen inches nearly everywhere. About a mile from camp, around eleven in the morning, I climbed a twenty-foot cliff over a deep pool below a long, shallow riffle. Pete waded as far as he could up a narrow gravel bar at the tail of the pool and then began to make short casts over the deeper water. My spot was perfect to watch from, nearly straight above the best-looking water, the sun behind me illuminating every rock and pebble on the bottom.

Pete landed and released a couple of fair-sized trout with his short casts. Then, on his first cast over the heart of

·

the pool, two huge trout came up for his fly at once. Most of the large trout in Mill Creek rise slowly for a fly and suck it in with calm confidence. These two, which appeared from beneath a wide ledge directly below me the instant the fly touched water, raced for the fly, shooting upward so force- fully that each broke the surface with a vicious slash. Pete jerked back on the rod instinctively, but both fish had missed the fly.

"Did you see them?" I asked stupidly.

"Are you kidding?"

"Try again."

He did, several times, drifting the big fly down over the ledge, but neither fish showed again. "How big were they?" Pete called to me when he'd given up.

"Big," I said. I thought about it. Looking down at fish, as I had been, makes them appear smaller than they are.

"How big?"

"Well, one was quite a bit bigger than the other. I'd guess the small one was twenty inches."

We killed one large trout for dinner, and Red Hawk, who had done well downstream, brought back one of his own. He had also found half a dozen arrowheads—the small, intricately carved bird points—in front of a small cave on the north bank.

Once again we talked about Ishi by the fire, which we fed with small logs of scrub oak.

"I think he'd have stayed," I said, "if there'd been one other person alive here for company. A woman. Another man. A child. It wouldn't have mattered. Somebody, though. When his last friend or family member died, he couldn't take it anymore."

"They had a hard life," Red Hawk said. "That Lassen Trail is pretty close. Can you imagine what it was like for the Yahis when the whites first arrived here? Imagine if a spaceship landed in some town. Not just one, but dozens, hundreds. That's what the covered wagons must have looked like to the Yahis. And they were full of people who'd kill Indians just for fun."

"Why couldn't they have left the Yahis alone?" Pete asked. "What did they want with this land down here?"

"They wanted to kill Indians," Red Hawk said. "That's pretty much what they wanted."

Once again we talked about fishing; mostly, I think, because it was a happier subject. We all agreed that the trout came up recklessly between ten o'clock and two. Before ten, there were few—if any—grasshoppers on the water. After two, the trout were too gorged to bother feed-

·

ing. "I killed my fish just before two," Red Hawk told us, "and it was so full of grasshoppers that its stomach looked like a rubber balloon stuffed full of coat hangers."

We went to bed a little earlier than the night before and got up a little earlier to fish again. Though fishing wasn't at its best before ten, it was good enough.

But Pete and I were careful to time it so that we arrived at the pool of the two large trout at about ten-thirty, hoping that their appetites had been whetted by then, but that they still had plenty of room in their stomachs for more.

Pete tried for them again, and I climbed the cliff to watch.

False-casting, the orange line snaking smoothly back and forth in a tight loop, he worked out thirty feet of line, and then dropped the big fly gently to the barely riffled surface of the pool. One of the trout—the larger one—came up as hard as it had the day before, slashing through the surface, even showing its tail, throwing rainbow spray a yard. But it missed the fly again, and Pete, who had set the hook into nothing and yanked it away, swore.

"Put it right back," I said.

He did—three times—but neither fish moved. I could see that he'd given up hope when he stripped off another yard of line and lackadaisically cast again. The second trout came up slowly to meet the fly, open mouth showing white when it was halfway there. Without disturbing the surface, it sucked the fly in and started down lazily—and then it felt the hook.

For the next few minutes, the pool was a lively place. The trout did everything a trout can do, but I knew that it was well hooked, and that all Pete had to do was take his

·

time. He did, and landed a rainbow slightly more than twenty inches long and as big around at the middle as a well-inflated football. I'm sure of the length because I measured the fish carefully against my rod before we released it.

We headed upstream, figuring we'd try for the bigger trout on our way back to camp that afternoon. At least a mile above camp, farther than we'd gone the day before, we found a cave at a sharp bend in the stream. The opening was cut into the base of a steep cliff about fifty yards up a gentle, brushy slope from the water.

The ceiling had been blackened by centuries of campfire smoke, and no less than half a dozen grinding bowls were scattered about on the dusty floor. In a corner, coated with the fine brown dust, I found a small, perfectly shaped mortar and left it there beside one of the bowls, certain I would find it again on another trip.

Pete and I sat on rocks near the mouth of the cave and talked about the Yahis who had used this shelter. Ishi himself had certainly been here. He and many other Yahis—generations of them—had sat here on these same comfortable rocks by their fires through rainy winter days. They

had ground acorns in the stone bowls, made their bows and arrowheads, then killed their deer on the flatlands above the canyon walls. The bird points Red Hawk had found were for quail, and, during the fall and winter, migrating flocks of band-tailed pigeons and mourning doves. They killed trout, too, at this time of year, probably luring them up to the surface with live grasshoppers floated downstream and then spearing the fish from above and behind them.

"It must have been good," Pete said.

"It was hard sometimes, too. It was hard most of the time."

"So what? That's part of what *made* it good."

"I agree."

"It made a lot more sense than the lives most people live now."

"I agree," I said. "But my colleagues would call you a 'romantic primitivist.'"

"Who cares what they'd say?"

"I don't."

Before we left to head upstream we sat for a while without talking, feeling the presence of Yahi people with us in the cave.

·

In a pool a few hundred yards farther upstream, we learned what the eventual fate of Mill Creek's trout will be.

In about six feet of water over a level bedrock bottom, we saw at least two dozen eighteen-inch fish holding near the surface in the gentle current.

"Are those trout?" Pete asked.

"What else could they be? Go on. Cast. Put it up above them."

"You cast. I had the chance at the big ones down below."

I dropped the grasshopper fly about twenty feet above the school of fish and we watched it float slowly down.

One of them started up for the fly, then changed its mind and drifted back down. A second fish and then a third did exactly the same thing.

"I need a lighter leader on this slow water," I said.

But as soon as I'd said it, a fish near the bottom end of the school rose and took the fly, the ring of the take spreading across the calm water.

When I set the hook, I expected a trout to jump and then run, but nothing happened. I reeled the line tight enough to bow the rod, and still nothing happened. I cranked the fish in.

"What is it?" Pete asked.

"A squawfish. But don't ask me why they call them that."

I killed it to eat and to get it out of the stream, but I knew it wouldn't help much.

When I cleaned it, I showed Pete the young trout in its stomach.

"The native trout won't last very long now," I said. "These things came up out of the Sacramento River. They

·

like warm water, so when they drained Mill Creek down in the valley, the water temperature went way up and attracted these things. These aren't even big ones. They get huge, and they multiply fast, and they eat everything in sight."

We talked about it by the fire that night, and agreed it was an old chain of predictable events, of constant flux and constant loss. The white men had driven the Yahis out, ending with Ishi. The salmon and steelhead were gone now, because of reduced stream flows in the Sacramento Valley. Red Hawk had thought that at least the wild trout would survive in healthy numbers, so long as they were killed sparingly; but now they, too, would disappear, and there was nothing anyone could do about it. To add a final and distasteful irony, someone had insultingly given the fish that would finally decimate the last resident native creatures in Yahi country an Indian name.

That night as I lay awake thinking about it, several satellites streaked across the black patch of sky over the canyon.

After breakfast the next morning, we hiked up the steep canyon wall and then along the rocky ridge past digger pines and sunbaked oaks to the jeep.

7

. . .

Preferences

*. . . we preferred the hunt to a life
of idleness, bickerings and jealousies.*

——Crazy Horse

Granddad Brant taught me to shoot with an old single-shot
.22 rifle, the one he told me was mine the night he died.

During our early lessons, he would place a tin can on a
tree stump and then move away to a safe distance while I

.

tried to hit it. For targets we used Log Cabin maple syrup cans shaped like cabins with chimneys that served as spouts. Gradually—about five yards at a time—he moved me farther back from the tree stump. When I could hit the can nearly every time at a range of about fifty yards, Granddad told me to aim at the spout of the can, to try to hit the chimney. When I could hit the chimney two times out of three, we moved on to the final stage in my lessons.

"Shooting at cans is a game, Mikey," he said. "What you have to learn now is to think *hard* about shooting. You have to really *aim*. Later on, when you hunt, you have to know what you're aiming at, and you have to be able to hit it in the right place."

He walked into the barn and soon came back out with an old wide-brimmed hat in his hand. "Load up," he said.

I took a long-rifle cartridge out of my pocket, slid it into the chamber, and closed the gun. Because it was a single-shot, the hammer had to be cocked to make it ready to fire.

Granddad Brant walked out into the field that was lined on three sides with the red raspberry bushes. When he was about thirty yards away, he turned to face me and held the old hat out at arm's length.

"Now take careful aim and hit the hat," he said. "Hit the big part of the hat."

•

I was afraid to do it. "What if I hit you?" I said.

"If you hit me, it's my fault. I'm the one who taught you to shoot."

"I don't want to hit you, though," I said.

"You won't," he said. "Don't worry, Mikey. I'm not crazy."

"Do you really want me to do it?"

"Go ahead. It's just a hat. Aim and shoot."

I raised the rifle to my shoulder, cocked it, then aimed very carefully and fired. I hit the hat, dead center. Grand-dad Brant looked at it and smiled.

For the rest of that summer, Granddad Brant held the hat and I shot it until there wasn't much of it left.

That was his last summer, and it was the first time that he talked to me about hunting.

"Nobody has to hunt to live anymore," he told me in the barn, as he sipped some bourbon after one of our last shooting lessons. As a joke, he had placed the mutilated old hat on the skull on the shelf behind him. "But you'll want to hunt. You'll have to for different reasons than the Mohawks had. It's in your blood, I can tell that already. It's a healthy thing to have. You have it."

·

. . .

Isolation

How much wildness is enough? How much is possible?

I decided to spend a week alone in remote country. I wanted to feel the isolation Ishi had experienced when he finally found himself alone in the Mill Creek canyon. It

.

would also tell me how much real wildness I could take myself.

I chose a roadless, thickly wooded area in the Cascade Mountains, about a hundred miles north of our home, and consisting of steep slopes and ridges and a few fair-sized creeks that cut narrow valleys through the country.

At noon on a clear day in mid-October, I parked in a grassy clearing several yards off a rural two-lane road, followed a narrow trail through an old-growth stand of Douglas firs and cedars, found a creek at the end of the trail and started to hike up it. Though much smaller than Mill Creek, I knew the stream would hold native fish.

I wore a wide-brimmed hat, a sweatshirt, jeans, and an old pair of Nikes, with a warm jacket knotted around my waist by the sleeves. I carried a single-shot 20-gauge shotgun and had a hunting knife and hatchet in my belt. In my pocket were a dozen matches I had waterproofed by dipping the heads in hot wax, two shotgun shells, ten feet of six-pound-test fishing line and two small hooks stuck into an old wine-bottle cork. Nothing more.

The creek was lovely, flowing clear among moss-covered gray boulders. Fallen maple leaves, some still golden and some rotted black, lay thick along the banks and floated on the water, moving down with the gentle current to collect in eddies. More leaves fell as I worked my way upstream, bright golden in shafts of sunlight through the branches.

There wasn't much sunlight, though. The maples and alders were dense along the creek, with hundred-foot-tall firs and cedars close behind them. Before I'd traveled a quarter-mile, I was worried. There had been some rain in

·

September and early October. Though the skies had been
clear for several days, the woods remained sodden. My
shoes and pants legs were soon soaked, and I could see my
breath when I exhaled. Dry firewood—and kindling to
start it burning—might be hard to find.

My first priority, before fire and wood, was shelter, a
place to keep me dry if it rained. Hiking along the creek
was slow going, but after a couple of miles and an hour or so
had passed, I found what I wanted. High water had carved
a depression four or five feet deep into the creek's west

·

bank, forming a small cave. The floor of the cave was dry
and fairly flat, but rocky, and the roof, laced with tree roots,
appeared to be stable. A few yards below the depression, a
cedar tree had fallen straight across the stream, and drift-
wood had collected behind it, creating a logjam and a pool
about four feet deep where several small trout were holding, dark-backed and clearly visible against a bedrock
bottom.

I wanted to fish, but my next obligation was to find a
good spot for a fire and then kindling and wood to make it.
I climbed up the steep bank, looking for a clearing where
the sun might have dried some twigs or pinecones. Already
I was lonely enough to wish I'd brought the dog along.

Though I didn't much like to admit it to myself, I was
vaguely frightened, too. For one of the few times in my life,
no one knew where I was. Even I didn't know exactly
where I was. I'd told Hilde the general area I'd be in; but if
it came to any sort of disaster, a search party would be lucky
to find me—or what was left of me—by Christmas. And
that was how I wanted it. There was no other way to come
anywhere near the sense of isolation Ishi must have felt.

Soon the strain of the climb wiped all such thoughts
away, for a while. Blazing a tree trunk every forty or fifty
yards with my hatchet—I wanted to be able to find my cave
in a hurry in case of bad weather—I climbed about a thou-
sand feet in half an hour, and sweat was pouring off me by
the time I reached a narrow game trail that continued
upward through the old-growth trees. It was so steep here
that even the deer used switchbacks. Before I'd gone very
far, I came across a dead doe, a recent killing. Both
hindquarters had been gnawed away, and so had the stom-

ach all the way up to the exposed ribs, white and shiny-wet against the floor of the forest. Either coyotes or a cougar must have done it.

After another half-hour of climbing, my thigh muscles feeling the strain, I saw that some of the big firs were scarred black from an old fire. One of the largest of them had come down in a storm, its huge tangle of roots just a few yards off the game trail on the downhill side. Not far beyond the fallen tree, the fire had burned a four- or five-acre clearing, which was now overgrown with brush, including a number of good-sized elderberry bushes. I could eat the ripe berries, and I was sure that blue grouse would feed there on the berries, too. Between an elderberry bush and the fire-scarred trees of the border of the forest, I found a few feet of level ground at the base of an outcropping of rock. It was a good place to build a fire, to sleep, and, as well as I could figure it, to catch the early-morning sun.

I lay my shotgun, my jacket, the shotgun shells, and my box of matches at the base of the outcropping, then searched for kindling. In twenty minutes, I'd gathered a supply of dry sticks that would probably last me three or four days. As I collected the sticks, I noticed small grasshoppers perched on twigs and on the rocky earth itself, lethargic now in the cool October weather, and I swatted about a dozen of them with my hat, killing them without crushing them, then slid them carefully into the same loose pocket that held the hooks and fishing line.

I made three trips back down the slope to the fallen fir tree, hacking chunks of the thick, dried bark from the underside and carrying them back in heavy armloads to stack beside the kindling. When I finally started back down

•

to the creek to fish for my dinner, I felt pleasantly secure. I had a temporary home and the means to heat it.

But when I passed the dead doe, another wave of the vague fear went through me. I stopped by the carcass and looked behind me, then all around. It was afternoon now, and dark in the shade of the forest. All I could see were tall, silent trees.

It's always surprising how little effort and time it takes to get down a hill that was real work to climb. There were at least two hours of daylight left when I reached the creek, and that would give me about an hour to fish, if I needed it.

I didn't need that much time, but I used it anyway, which turned out to be a mistake. With a hook clinch-knotted to the end of my carefully coiled ten-foot line, I made my way upstream, sneaking up on the small pools, which were separated by stretches where the water flowed only inches deep between the boulders. Most of the pools were no more than three or four feet across and two feet deep; while a few, usually those formed behind logjams and beneath falls, were several yards across and as deep as five or six feet. The largest pools held the most and biggest fish, and I knew from the start that these were trout that had never seen men.

Each time I dropped a grasshopper onto the surface, several trout shot up at the bait. It was only a question of which fish would reach it first. I killed two seven-inchers in the first place I tried. Even when I came out from behind a boulder and stood over the pool in plain sight, the remaining trout came up again and again when I dropped the bait onto the water. I pulled it away before they could reach it;

·

but when I dropped it back, they rose again, the smallest fish coming up a dozen times or more before they tired of it. I fished as many as two dozen pools, either releasing the fish I hooked or pulling the bait away before they could take it.

I kept thinking I'd turn back after one more spot, make the climb, start a fire, and cook my dinner. But, as always happens, the next pool upstream looked promising—and the next, and the next. Finally I came to a pool at the base of a three-foot waterfall that really was the best one yet. It was about fifteen feet long, ten feet across, and at least eight feet deep, with a gravel-covered bottom and a bedrock ledge along its far side. I was certain there would be at least one big trout holding somewhere underneath that ledge.

I climbed up onto a boulder to see whether I could throw a grasshopper far enough to reach the ledge, and I nearly made it. The hopper landed beyond midstream, and a rainbow trout of twelve or fourteen inches came out of the shadows and started up hard for it.

But in making the long toss, I'd leaned so far forward that I lost my balance. Swaying on top of the rounded boulder, my left arm waving wildly while my right hand gripped the line, I watched the trout rise, the water so clear he appeared to be swimming through air. But it was water, all right—ice cold. I fell face forward off the rock and into the pool.

This creek was fed by early snowmelt from the high country. The water temperature couldn't have been much above forty-five degrees. When I thrashed my way out of the water, I was gasping for breath, then shivering, then swearing. I still had the line in my hand, but I hadn't hooked the trout. Of course I felt like a fool, but not simply

·

because I'd fallen in. The real mistake had been fishing for sport when meat was what I needed.

Soaking wet, I climbed back up the mountainside, moving at least twice as fast as I had the first time. When I reached the sharp bend where I'd seen the dead doe, I thought I might be lost because it wasn't there. I kept going a couple of minutes, until I was absolutely certain that had been the right spot, and then I jogged back down for another look. I could see where the carcass had been, and I could also see where it had been dragged away, uphill across the trail and into the trees. Then I knew I was sharing the mountainside with a resident cougar.

I was badly chilled, shaking all over, by the time I reached my clearing.

Shielding the flame carefully, I managed to start a fire with my first match, then added progressively larger sticks of kindling and finally wedged a slab of the bark against the rock outcropping, directly over the small blaze. I blew on it gently through cupped hands, and after a minute or two the bark began to smoke, then sputter so I could barely hear it. Finally the edges burst up into bright orange flame.

By the time the fire was blazing, night had fallen. I squatted, naked except for my jacket, drying my clothes from the inside out: underwear and socks first, then jeans and undershirt, then my hat and my shoes. I had wrung things out as best I could and held them over the fire on sticks.

The nylon shoes dried quickly. Everything else took a long time, especially the sweatshirt. As the clothing

·

steamed, there was nothing to do but think. As I would learn through the following days and nights, there isn't any way to avoid thinking when you're all alone. When immediate needs have been satisfied—and perhaps some future needs as well—there are few distractions. Ishi must have become a philosopher toward the end of his life in Yahi country, because he had no choice.

When I was finally dressed again, I roasted my trout, using one of the sticks I'd dried my clothes on. I ate the fish and thought about the cougar. I'd glimpsed one in the wild on a bird-hunting trip and heard one on a long run through the mountains, screaming from a rocky bluff above me. They were shy animals, but even the remote possibility of an encounter scared me. It wasn't likely—in fact, it was next to impossible—but the idea of it scared me anyway. It's easy to be sure of things at home, or with company, but not quite so easy all alone.

The shotgun lay at my side, the two bright yellow shells beside it. Because it was a single shot, the hammer had to be cocked before the gun would fire. I felt like a fool again, but I loaded it and tested the well-oiled hammer two or three times with my thumb.

When I'd finished eating, I tossed the remains of the trout into the darkness as far from my campsite as I could. I could have burned the bones, but I was afraid the aroma drifting with smoke might attract the cougar. After placing two large slabs of bark across the fire, I tried to sleep. I lay on my back, watching the stars, and finally dozed off.

No more than half an hour could have passed when I woke up terrified, my stomach turning over, my heart pounding in my ears. Twenty or thirty yards behind me,

·

something large was moving through the trees. I'd heard it through my sleep. In an instant, I was on my knees, facing that way, gun in my hands and hammer cocked. It must have been a deer heading down the steep slope to the creek for water, but I stayed there gripping the cocked gun until it was well out of hearing range.

There was nothing to be frightened of—this was certainly a safer place than a cheap hotel room off Columbus Circle in New York—but it was half an hour before I felt relaxed enough, secure enough, to lie back down and try to sleep. With three more slabs of bark crisscrossed on the bed of the fire, I stretched out on my side to warm my back. Somewhere, far away on another mountain, coyotes howled. Finally I dozed off again, but I don't think I slept for more than twenty minutes at a stretch throughout the night.

I got up when the first sunlight hit me. The rocky ground had me stiff and sore in a lot of places, and I spent half an hour exploring the clearing and eating dry, sour elderberries for breakfast.

I decided to try to kill a grouse, so I picked up the loaded shotgun and started around the clearing at a slow walk. First I circled it—the old theory, taught to me by Granddad Brant, is that birds become confused and are apt to sit tightly in their cover when they hear sounds coming at them from all directions—and then I began to walk slowly uphill through the elderberry bushes, stopping every ten or fifteen feet. Another strategy, also learned from Granddad Brant, and I know this one works, holds that pausing that way frightens the birds—perhaps because they think a predator is setting itself to pounce—and flushes them from

·

cover. Things happened exactly as planned. These were the blue grouse I'd expected—big, relatively slow birds—and half a dozen of them thundered into flight before I was halfway up the clearing. The last of them was the low, straightaway shot I'd been waiting for—I wanted to use only one of my shells—and I killed it cleanly.

Back at the fire, I cleaned the bird, its craw stuffed with elderberries, and tossed the insides far down the hill for some animal to find. Then I skinned and roasted it over a hot fire. The tender breast meat tasted delicious, but the legs were so tough and stringy that they were difficult to chew.

After the meal, I used some soft side feathers to create a lure. By tying a hook to the end of my line with a turle knot, I could tighten the loop of the knot around the ends of the soft inch-long feathers so that they lay straight back against the shank of the hook, forming what amounted to a very crude streamer fly. That afternoon, down at the creek, I hooked and released at least two dozen trout and killed three others for my evening meal, each from a different pool.

The first full day set the pattern for the routine of those that followed: a morning forage for firewood, food, and water, then periods of exploration and sleep. Each day when my chores were done, I hiked through the mountains, and I saw a lot of country and a lot of life: hawks, ospreys, a golden eagle, several deer, including a five-point buck, a civet cat, and countless blue and ruffed grouse and mountain quail—but no cougar.

The weather held through the week. At night, temperatures went down into the low forties. From the third night

·

on, when my irrational fears had subsided and I began to sleep reasonably well, the fire would burn out and I would wake in the early morning stiff and aching from cold. I began talking to myself on the third day. By the evening of the fourth day, I was fighting off depression.

What got me through the rest of the week was knowing I could leave when it was over.

On my last morning, I thought about killing another grouse but decided against it and started home with a shotgun shell and three matches left over. Stiff and sore, tired and dirty, I was very much looking forward to seeing people.

Back down at the creek, I stopped long enough to go after the big trout, but not with one of my grouse-feather streamer flies. I used a grasshopper, kept my balance on the boulder, and landed a lovely fish, firm and bright, its lateral line the color of a dark red rose, its back and fins speckled black.

After I admired the fish, I twisted the hook from its jaw and lowered it back into the pool. The trout went back to its life and I returned to mine, with a clearer understanding of both Ishi and my own limitations.

. . .

Indian

Summer

Once when we were sitting in the barn, while I was holding the old skull in my hands, I asked Granddad Brant how Chief Joseph Brant had died.

"Noss thinks it was his heart, Mikey. He's read everything there is about it. I guess there weren't any doctors

.

around back then, at least not for Joseph—or maybe he didn't want any—but his wife Catherine wrote about it and it sounded like a heart attack to your Uncle Noss."

"How old was he?"

"Sixty-four."

"Is that pretty old?"

"I'm a lot older. But back then it was pretty old. I think about him pretty much these days. Right up until the end, he did the best he could for the Mohawks. But I think by the time he died, he knew for sure the Mohawks would have to learn to live like white people sooner or later. To live like them *some* of the time."

I stared at the skull, and I tried to imagine that once it had been a living person. I could imagine that more easily than I could accept the possibility that I would be dead, too, someday.

"He died in the fall, Mikey, and the weather was what they call Indian summer. Do you know what some Indians called heaven?"

"The happy hunting grounds."

"That tells you something, doesn't it?"

"Did he die at his house?"

"At his farm up there in Canada. He knew he was dying, so they took him outside. That was where he wanted to be. I have the papers Catherine wrote about it. The geese were flying south then—big flocks in those days—and that must have been one of the last things he heard. You've heard the geese going over."

"Sure," I said.

"Maybe it was the last thing he heard." Granddad Brant smiled, thinking about it. "That part must have been nice."

•

10

...

The

Completed

Circle

People get into language, dance and songs and stuff, powwows, and they think that's culture. How much of the Quinalt culture is left? I see about two hundred and fifty people—they're fishing, they're happy, they're doing what our ancestors did. They get their deer, they get their elk. They live the way they want to live. That's more culture than the powwow dancing thing.

——Quinalt leader Joe Delacruz

In December 1993 one of the cable television networks produced two movies about American Indians: *Geronimo* and *The Broken Chain*. *The Broken Chain* purported to portray the life of Joseph Brant and concentrated on his relation-

·

ship with his brother during the period ending with the defeat of the British and Joseph's subsequent forced exile to Canada.

The movie's obvious message was that Joseph Brant was "too white"—that he put too much trust in the British, adopted too many of their ways, and that this was his failure and his downfall. Perhaps he *was* "too white," and perhaps I have been too, in my own life, but I prefer to believe that both of us, and John Brant along with us, were merely facing obvious and inevitable truths.

The purity of Mohawk life was doomed more than two hundred years ago. Ishi struggled alone out of the Mill Creek canyon more than eighty years ago. When I visit Mill Creek—and I've been back there many times, with both Pete and Hilde—I can dearly love what remains of the country and envy the old Yahi ways, but I can't very well forget that I'm within a long day's walk of one of America's busiest interstate freeways. (And the most amazing and depressing thing about it is that it's all happened so very quickly—I watched satellites sail across the night sky from the same sandy beach on Mill Creek where the last wild Indian lived when my Grandfather Brant was a middle-aged man.)

My own brief attempt at living in the wild was, at best, a limited success. After all, I've grown up riding in cars, enjoying central heating, listening to radios, eating prepared foods, even watching television. I often use nylon tents and propane stoves and lanterns when I camp, and I catch fish with graphite fly rods. I train my own hunting dogs, but I've never yet seen a wolf. Without a surviving oral tradition, I read and write.

·

An Indian named Okute summed it up this way: "Now our horses require a mixture of food; they have less endurance and require constant care. It is the same with the Indians; they have less freedom, and they fall easy prey to disease. In the old days they were rugged and healthy, drinking pure water and eating the meat of the buffalo..."

I've tried to live up to my Mohawk blood, and I've passed what I know and believe in on to my children. And now, with the birth of her son, our daughter Ingrid has given us another generation.

Billy is only a little past four months old as I write this; but, with the help of a comfortable pack, I've already been able to take him with me to good places.

I know an old Indian campsite on the western slopes of the Cascades, a little hunting camp in a place remote enough so that it's possible that no one besides me—and now Billy—has been there in more than a hundred years. It is on a flat, triangular-shaped meadow of five or six acres enclosed on all sides by huge white oak trees, interspersed with old-growth ponderosa pines, some of their rough-barked, cinnamon-colored trunks a hundred feet tall. Two steep-banked, rock-bottomed creeks that surely once held good runs of fish—just as Mill Creek did—converge at the east end of the meadow. Elk use that country in winter, signs of deer are everywhere all year round, and big coveys of mountain quail can often be heard running through the dried-out oak leaves near the creeks. Band-tailed pigeons feed on acorns in the fall, and ruffed grouse roost in the oak-tree branches.

.

In the spring of the year, six tepee rings are just barely visible—shallow circular depressions about twenty feet in diameter—with some of the rocks that were used to wall in the dwellings still scattered about. Evidence of fire pits is still there, too: charred stones, bits of charcoal, blackened earth, and fragments and splinters of bone. Along with the bone pieces, the blackened earth holds chips of obsidian, jasper, and agate.

After late winter or early spring rains have washed away some topsoil is the best time to explore the old camp for artifacts, and I hiked in with Billy in March.

All across the meadow the thick grass had begun to green, with the creeks flowing high and slightly colored from snowmelt. The healthy pines were the same shade of green as the grass, but the oaks wouldn't come into leaf for another month or more. Mountain quail could be nesting now, or would be very soon, in thick buck brush above the creek banks. It was cool in the shade, but surprisingly warm in the sunlight, as I walked slowly around the campground perimeter, with Billy at least half-asleep and secure against my chest in his pack.

The first arrowhead I saw, an obsidian bird point, was

lodged against the protruding root of a ponderosa pine near the converging creeks, where it had probably washed from higher ground. It had not been finished, though it had no flaws that I could see. I bent and picked it up, careful not to disturb Billy. When I held it up to the light between his face and mine for closer examination, it still seemed perfect.

As always, when I handle something sacred, I wondered who had made it and how long it took. What did he look like, and what kind of life did he live? Did he have his children here in this camp, one of them perhaps as young as Billy? How old was he when he last set foot here, and how and when did he die? When was the camp last used, and why didn't he finish the bird point? It was possible he had left the unfinished point behind when the last people here were disrupted and forced to flee for their lives by whites from a nearby mining town.

I dropped the bird point back on the ground, then slid it with the toe of my boot as close as I could to exactly where it had come from, up against the tree root.

As I walked back up the meadow, I imagined how life must have been lived here. From the location of the tepee rings and the creeks and the way the land lay, it was clear how the Indians had fished and hunted, where they had cleaned and butchered their animals and dried their fish, where they had cooked and bathed and sat to pass an hour or two on a warm, sunny morning.

A Steller's jay, imitating a hawk, as they often do, called from high in a ponderosa. Wind moved steadily through the tops of the pines. "How do you like it here, Billy?" I asked.

He opened one eye, half-smiled, then sighed and closed his eye and slept again, breathing deeply.

•

Near the top of the meadow, a few feet from an old white oak, was a fallen log so weather-beaten and worn with age that it must have been used by the Indians. I sat there with Billy still asleep in his pack.

With luck and health, my grandson will live most of his life in the twenty-first century, a century I can honestly say I'll be glad to mostly miss. He'll probably have to know about computers, about something called an "information superhighway," about modems and megabytes, whatever they are.

The last man who had used the fallen log we sat on had very different concerns. It might have been the same man who never quite finished the bird point I'd found. In this camp he must have made bows and arrow shafts as well as points, because it was a hunting camp, and all the required ingredients were available here: wood, fish, deer, and, in fall, flocks of Canada geese passing down toward the valley on their southward flight. To make a hunting bow, the wood of the shaft had to be seasoned in sunlight for at least three weeks. The back tendon from a deer's leg was soaked in water overnight and then peeled down to threadlike strips, which could be turned into long strings of white glue by vigorous chewing. First, another glue was made by boiling fish skins and the bone marrow into a paste. Coating the bow with a thin layer of this fish-skin–bone-marrow paste and then carefully chewing and winding the strips of sinew around it gave the wood its resiliency and strength. More strings of the sinew, wetted and then intricately interwoven, formed the bowstring. Arrow shafts were strengthened by the same boiled paste and chewed sinew, and the

·

goose-wing feathers were both waterproof and straight, so that a well-aimed arrow would fly true.

Were these less significant skills than learning computer commands?

Billy awakened, and I lifted him out of the pack. I still had half an hour before I would need to leave for town and get him back home to be fed.

He is a strong, healthy, happy boy with reddish hair and shining eyes. When I balanced him on my knee, he smiled at me, kicked his feet and waved his arms, and then, attracted by the brightness, stared wide-eyed toward the creek at the camp's eastern border where bright patches of sunlight struck the ground.

"I guess maybe I'll be the old man in your life," I told him. "I hope I can be as good as the one I had."

Before that time comes, I'll have to figure out what to say. How much bad news should I try to tell him, and where should I begin? Billy, his thin hair moved by the wind, legs still kicking and chubby arms waving wildly now, stared smiling at the sunlight as random thoughts of

·

both the past and his twenty-first-century future drifted through my mind: *In my lifetime the population of the world has tripled, and in his it will double for sure and possibly triple again—and this with many rivers and forests dead or dying already. In southern California thousands of Juaneno Indians lie buried and forgotten underneath parking lots, freeways, and shopping malls. Pretty soon, according to news reports, Indian reservations—the ones that haven't built gambling casinos—will become the repositories for nuclear waste.*

The Steller's jay called again, this time in its own natural voice. Startled, Billy looked upward toward the sound. "I'll start off by teaching you about birds," I told him. "First the ones that come into town, and then the better ones, out here. After that come the fish and animals. Later on we'll camp in the woods, and by good rivers and lakes. Maybe we'll go to Mill Creek together and camp in one of the caves. I can show you how to call in wild ducks and turkeys, if you want, and to cast and tie your own flies. You should read some good, true books—Black Elk, Thoreau, Leopold, lots of other ones—but they can wait until later. I'll tell you about Joseph and John Brant and about the Mohawks."

Two good things happened on the hike back out of the campsite. Near the middle of the meadow, close to another fallen log, I found the broken tip of another obsidian bird point. When I put the point into Billy's little hand, he gripped it and smiled. Then, when he let go, it landed so close to where I had found it that I didn't even have to move it with my boot. Beyond the meadow, on a hillside of oaks, a big ruffed grouse burst out of ground cover nearly at my feet and flew across the hillside, veering through the oak trees. That unexpected, sudden explosive drumming of wings can frighten adults, but all Billy did was blink and strain to turn his head to see where the sound had come from. I couldn't have asked for a better sign than that.

When we reached the top of that hill, I could see the town we had to return to, far away and far below us, in the valley haze through a narrow gap in the mountains.

•